FASCINATING NEWS STORIES

A READING COMPREHENSION SKILL BUILDER

Fred Pyrczak and Daniel Levine

illustrated by Gene Fuller

J. Weston Walch, Publisher
Portland, Maine

2   3   4   5   6   7   8   9   10

ISBN 0-8251-0107-7

Contents

To the Teacher

Fascinating News Stories presents high-interest news stories from national wire services as well as regional newspapers and periodicals.

Reading comprehension questions accompany each article. The questions help students develop all of the major reading comprehension skills they need in order to become mature readers. The questions are grouped and clearly labeled according to the skills they help develop; thus, students can easily recognize the purpose of each set of questions.

THE SKILLS. For each article, there are questions that require the application of these three skills:

1. developing vocabulary knowledge, including the use of context in many cases;

2. achieving literal comprehension (remembering facts);

3. drawing implications (discussing reactions and insights).

In addition, clearly labeled sets of questions requiring the application of two or more of the subsequent skills follow each article:

4. identifying main ideas,

5. drawing inferences,

6. following structure and organization,

7. scanning the information,

8. identifying the sequence of events,

9. interpreting figures of speech,

10. identifying author's tone and purpose.

ORGANIZATION OF THE QUESTIONS. The Prereading Activities, which precede each article, are divided into three sections.

The first, "Making Predictions," asks students to use the title and their everyday knowledge in order to predict facts, points of view, etc., that they are likely to find in the article. This section helps students develop a purpose for reading. The first section of the Postreading Activities reminds students to check their predictions.

The second section of the Prereading Activities, "Understanding New Words," contains questions that promote vocabulary knowledge. In many cases, students are referred to the context of the article to derive meanings. Teachers may also wish to allow students to use dictionaries for this section.

The last Prereading Activities section, "Focusing Your Reading," suggests specific information that students should look for and evaluate while they read. The first question under "Discussing Your Reactions and Insights" after each article asks students for this information and their evaluation of it.

The Postreading Activities after each article also contain sets of questions that develop two or more of skills four through ten previously listed. The line numbers on the right margin of each news story will help students to answer many of these questions.

INTEGRATING READING AND WRITING SKILL DEVELOPMENT. This book was conceived and written to be a systematic aid in developing reading comprehension skill. However, the authors are acutely aware of the desirability and efficiency of using a set of stimulus materials to develop both reading and writing skills. Thus, the articles for *Fascinating News Stories* were selected and many of the reading comprehension questions were written with this possibility in mind.

By having students respond with complete sentences to the "Remembering Facts" questions, which follow each article, teachers can promote knowledge of sentence construction. The questions under "Discussing Your Insights and Reactions," which also follow each article, provide the stimuli for having students write a paragraph or two. These questions ask students to express their opinions regarding specific issues raised in the articles.

In those classes in which an integrated approach to reading and writing skill development will be employed, it is especially important to have students read the student introduction, "To The Student," which points out that their teacher may modify the directions for some sets of questions for this purpose.

WHEN AND WHERE TO USE THIS BOOK. This book is designed for use with secondary and junior college students who need additional practice in developing literal comprehension skills while developing mature interpretation and evaluation skills.

While you and your students use this book, you will notice the rich language used in many of the articles. You will also notice that the articles are not watered-down, simplified versions of stories so common in reading development aids. With *Fascinating News Stories* your students will be dealing with real-life examples of fine North American journalism.

To the Student

This book presents real-life news stories that we hope you will find fascinating.

Before each article there are Prereading Activities that will help you establish a purpose for reading, help you understand difficult vocabulary, and help you focus your reading so that you'll notice the most important aspects of each article. Careful attention to these Prereading Activities will help you get the most out of this book.

Each article is followed by a number of questions that will help you develop mature reading comprehension skills. The line numbers on the right margin of each news story will help you to answer many of these questions.

Before each set of questions are directions that tell you how to answer them. However, since your teacher is in the best position to know exactly which skills you need to develop, he or she may make modifications in the directions. For example, it may be possible to answer some questions in a single word, yet your teacher may ask you to respond in complete sentences in order to give you practice in sentence and paragraph composition. It is important for you to pay special attention to any supplementary instructions your teacher gives so that your work is complete and satisfactory.

We wish you success in building your reading and writing skills. We've tried to select stories that will make your efforts both fascinating and fun.

Fred Pyrczak
Daniel Levine

Prereading Activities
SNAKE ATTEMPTS TO EAT MASTER

Part A MAKING PREDICTIONS. You will be reading a true story that has the title given above. Before you read the story, answer the following questions using information in the title and any hunches you may have.

1. Which of the following names is probably the name of the snake?

   A. J. Bennett Boggess   B. Monty   C. Rosemary Russell

2. Why did the snake probably attack?

   A. It was hungry and confused.

   B. It was trying to get free from captivity.

   C. It was angry or jealous.

3. After the attack, what did the master probably decide to do with the snake?

   A. punish it   B. have it retrained   C. get rid of it

Part B UNDERSTANDING NEW WORDS. Below are scrambled definitions of words used in the story you are about to read. Unscramble the definitions by rearranging the phrases. Phrases are separated by double slashes (//). Then write a sentence using each word.

4. **pythons** (noun) that crush their prey // snakes // very large, nonpoisonous // to death

5. **ornery** (adjective) ugly or mean // having // tendencies

6. **curator** (noun) a museum, library, etc. // in charge of // a person

7. **herpetology** (noun) having to do with // the branch // the study of reptiles and amphibians // of zoology

Part C FOCUSING YOUR READING. Now read the story. While you read, think about what you would have done if you had observed the events taking place.

Snake Attempts to Eat Master

Gainesville, Florida

The love affair is over between J. Bennett 1
Boggess and Monty because the 14-foot 2
python confused his master with dinner and 3
got as far as trying to swallow his head. 4

The python struck Boggess five times in 5
the forehead and wrapped itself around its 6
owner's head before unhinging its jaw and 7
starting to swallow. 8

After a bloody and violent struggle, Bog- 9
gess managed to get free from Monty's grasp. 10
He was later treated for shock at the Gaines- 11
ville hospital and had several snake teeth 12
pulled from his head. 13

As a result of the attack, Monty is now 14
kept under tighter security by Boggess and is 15
awaiting adoption by the Jacksonville Zoo. 16
Although Boggess said yesterday the animal 17
just became ornery, a Gainesville expert 18
thinks the python's behavior was in character. 19

"Snakes cannot be domesticated," said 20
Dr. Walter Auffenberg, curator of herpetology 21
at the Florida State Museum. "They are com- 22
pletely untrustworthy in that they can get 23
some cue from you that you're the food." 24

Boggess doesn't know what cue he sent 25
to Monty, a snake he bought five years ago 26
when it was only 26 inches long. It was 6 p.m. 27
and he was preparing to feed Monty the 28
usual meal of live rabbit. The python was 29
draped around his neck. 30

"I was sleeping when I heard this agoniz- 31
ing scream," said Rosemary Russell, Boggess' 32
girlfriend. When she came into the living 33
room, she said, she saw the most horrible 34
thing she's ever seen. 35

Monty was wrapped tightly around Bog- 36
gess' head, she said, digging its teeth into his 37
forehead. As she watched, the snake widened 38
its jaw to take in Boggess' entire head. 39

Richard Frank, Boggess' roommate, was 40
also present. 41

"Bennett fell back and grabbed the 42
snake's mouth," Frank remembered. As the 43
snake unhinged its jaw and wrapped itself 44
tighter around Boggess' head, "all you could 45
see was one eye and a nostril," Frank said. 46
"You could see the blood going down over 47
his eyes." 48

Both Russell and Frank were convinced 49
they had to kill the python before it killed 50
Boggess. But when they tried to pull the 51
snake away, it only tightened its grip. 52

Frank went to the kitchen to search for a 53
knife, while Russell went to look for an ax. 54

Suddenly, after being poked in the eyes 55
and mouth by Boggess, Monty relaxed his 56
grip. 57

"A snake doesn't have a very large brain," 58
Auffenberg said. "He gets all excited and 59

there's a warm moving thing that smells right 60
and zappo! That's it," he said. 61

Source: "Snake Attempts to Eat Master," Associated Press, 1981. Reprinted by permission of the publisher.

Postreading Activities
SNAKE ATTEMPTS TO EAT MASTER

Part A CHECKING YOUR PREDICTIONS. These are the answers to Part A of the *Prereading Activities:* 1. B, 2. A, 3. C
Which ones(s) did you get right?

Part B REMEMBERING FACTS. Answer the questions on a separate piece of paper. Try to answer without looking back at the story.

1. How long was the python at the time of the attack?
2. What did the python usually feed on?
3. At the hospital, what was pulled from the owners's head?
4. How many people are named in the passage?
5. The owner hopes to have the snake adopted by whom or what?
6. What weapons did the owner's friends plan to use against the snake?

Part C FOLLOWING STRUCTURE. Answer the following questions on a separate piece of paper. You may go back to the story.

7. To whom does "he" (line 11) refer?
8. To whom does "they" (line 23) refer?
9. What is the full name of the person whose "neck" is referred to in line 30?

Part D IDENTIFYING A MAIN IDEA. Answer the question by selecting the best choice. You may go back to the story.

10. Which of the following best expresses the main idea of the fifth paragraph (lines 20-24)?

   A. For expert advice on snakes, one should consult a herpetologist.
   B. It's not possible for humans to tame snakes.
   C. Snakes are very fond of food.

4

Part E DISCUSSING YOUR REACTIONS AND INSIGHTS. Consider these questions for possible discussion in the classroom.

11. How would you have felt and what would you have done if you were Boggess' friend and found him while he was being attacked by the snake?

12. Speculate on why some people keep dangerous animals as pets even when they know that it is risky to do so.

Prereading Activities
EXPLORER'S LIFETIME GOALS LIST:
It's 108 Down, Only 19 to Go

Part A MAKING PREDICTIONS. You will be reading a true story that has the title given above. Use your hunches to predict three of the many adventures the explorer has undertaken.

Part B UNDERSTANDING NEW WORDS. Below are words used in the story you are about to read. List them on a separate piece of paper. To the right of each word, write its meaning, selecting from the scrambled list.

Word
1. precocious
2. cremation
3. circumnavigate
4. elite
5. suffice
6. anthropologist
7. whimsy
8. inept

Meaning (listed in scrambled order)
A. a person whose work is to study the physical characteristics, social relationships, and customs of humans
B. to be more mature than is normal for one's age
C. the process of burning up, especially the process of burning a dead body
D. the group or part of a group thought to be the finest, best, most powerful, etc.
E. not capable; unequal to a task
F. to be sufficient or adequate
G. an odd fancy; idle notion or idea
H. to sail or fly around the earth, an island, etc.

Complete each of the following sentences by substituting one of the preceding words for the blank. The sentences are not part of the story but are given to help you understand the new words. (Do NOT write on this page. Rewrite the sentences on a separate piece of paper.)

9. It was just a _____, which I soon forgot all about.
10. The dead man's family decided on _____
11. She was a member of the _____ that ran the government from behind the scenes.
12. The _____child finished high school when he was 12 years old.
13. For our final adventure we decided to _____the globe.
14. The _____ went on a field trip to study a remote tribe.

15. The cook was so _____ that he burned just about everything.

16. She decided that it would _____ to write just a brief letter.

Part C FOCUSING YOUR READING. Now read the story. While you read, think about which of the adventures and activities you personally find most interesting. Why?

EXPLORER'S LIFETIME GOALS LIST:
It's 108 Down, Only 19 to Go

Canada, CA

Lots of people make lists, right? Grocery lists? Laundry lists? Lists to Get-Things-Done?

Then there is John Goddard, world champion list maker.

On a rainy Sunday afternoon 40 years ago, Goddard squeezed into the breakfast nook at his suburban Los Angeles home and made a list on a yellow legal pad.

It was 1940. He was 15, precocious, idealistic— and determined.

"Explore the Nile River, the Amazon River, the Congo River," his list began. "Climb Mt. Everest, Mt. Kilimanjaro, Mt. Fuji. Photograph Victoria Falls.

"Retrace travels of Marco Polo and Alexander the Great. Explore underwater the Red Sea. Visit the Taj Mahal and the Leaning Tower of Pisa."

"Land on and take off from an aircraft carrier. Watch a cremation cermony in Bali. Write a book. Run a mile in five minutes.

"Read the works of Shakespeare, Plato, Aristo-.... Become familiar with the compositions of Bach, Beethoven, Debussy. Light a match with a .22 rifle. Circumnavigate the globe."

In all Goddard listed 127 things he wanted to do in the course of his life.

Goddard is 56 now; no spring chicken, he. He prefers to be known as an "explorer" or "adventurer" rather than a maker of lists.

Yet his persistence, checking off item after item, ranks him among the traveled elite of the planet's 4,321,000,000 inhabitants.

Of his original 127 items, he checked off his 107th deed, No. 51, last summer, a visit to Easter Island in the Pacific Ocean. He added No. 69—ride a horse in the Rose Bowl Parade—on New Year's Day.

His most heroic feat: 4,162 miles down the Nile in a 15-foot kayak—where he shook scorpions out of his trousers, scraped clutches of leeches from his legs, got chased by a bull hippopotamus that snorted like a fairy-tale dragon, and discovered the African delicacies of gnats, pressed and dried into little cakes, roasted locusts, and boiled termites.

Submerged roots snagged the prow of his boat as he shot a rapids. "Instantly the torrent filled and engulfed it. I was dragged along upside down, my legs caught in the lashings which secured the duffel bags. I was drowning, and I knew it.

"Then my rifle fell loose and struck me full in the face, momentarily stunning me. As my senses returned, I gave one mighty heave in a desperate summoning of strength. Blessedly, I wrenched free of my deathtrap and fought to the surface."

A Congo River expedition fared worse. Goddard's companion, Briton Jack Yowell, vanished forever into a whirlpool. The journey of the Nile occurred in 1951. Twenty-eight years later, still working on his list, Goddard used it for a book, 348 pages, published last year by the Mormon Church's Brigham Young University Press.

Goddard's father was Mormon. He made a living as a financial wizard for a rich undertaker. Goddard makes a living as a lecturer, illustrating his life and hard times with films.

Goddard is not a rich man. That wasn't on his list. "Shoestring" financing sufficed for most of his deeds.

"People postpone living," he said the other day. "The excuses are 'not enough time, not enough talent, not enough money.' That's a cop-out on life. People say, 'I wish I had my life to live again.' Not me."

Among the check-offs of 40 years: "Dive in a submarine"—400 feet in the submarine USS Henhaden; "milk a poisonous snake"—a diamondback bit him; and "fly in a blimp, balloon, and glider."

Although Goddard leaves intact his 1940 list, he also improvises: 63,000 feet in an F-106 Delta Dart, a ride on a killer whale, bullfighter for a day in Colombia.

In his promotional brochure, Goddard, an anthropologist of sorts, casts himself as a "dynamic but unassuming" personality; in fact, he is a rather formal man, relatively humorless. He sees nothing funny about his toupee.

He is highly critical of the way "civilization is hooked into time frames. People are too hung up on dates, times. I can do anything now that I could do at 21," he asserts pointedly.

What Goddard does not dwell upon are his items unchecked. Item 93, "Appear in a Tarzan Movie," he dismisses as the whimsy of adolescence.

Item 66, "Visit every country in the world," becomes more complicated. In 40 years, the world added 60 countries.

Goddard has yet to make it to China to see the Great Wall and navigate the Yangtze River. And he discovered himself "embarrassingly inept" on item 114, "Compose music."

This does not mean he has given up. He hasn't. He is confident he will make item 127, "Live to the 21st Century," and he will not admit abject defeat on item 125, "Visit the moon."

Source: Gene Miller, "Explorer's Lifetime Goals List: It's 108 Down, Only 19 to Go," Knight-Ridder Newspaper Syndication, 1981. Reprinted by permission of the publisher.

Postreading Activities
EXPLORER'S LIFETIME GOALS LIST:
It's 108 Down, Only 19 to Go

Part A CHECKING YOUR PREDICTIONS.   Part A of the *Prereading Activities* asked you to predict three of the many adventures the explorer has undertaken.

How many of your predictions were correct?

Part B REMEMBERING FACTS.   Answer the following questions by selecting the best choice for each. Try to answer without looking back at the story.

1. In what year did Goddard first create his list?

    A. 1940   B. 1950   C. 1960

2. How old was Goddard when he first made his list?

    A. 10   B. 15   C. 20

3. Which of the following is one of the authors mentioned in the story?

    A. Bach   B. Shakespeare   C. Homer

4. What does Goddard prefer to be known as?

    A. a maker of lists
    B. an explorer or adventurer
    C. a religious leader

5. Which of the following has Goddard failed to do so far?

    A. Explore the Nile.
    B. Visit each country in the world.
    C. Visit Easter Island in the Pacific.

6. Which of the following has Goddard also failed to do so far?

    A. ride a horse in the Rose Bowl Parade
    B. explore the Congo River
    C. appear in a Tarzan movie

7. How does Goddard make his living?

    A. as an explorer
    B. as a lecturer
    C. as an artist

8. Goddard is referred to as a sort of

   A. psychologist.　　B. geologist.　　C. anthropologist.

9. Why does it become increasingly complicated for Goddard to reach his goal of visiting every country in the world?

   A. Because of political differences, some countries won't admit citizens of the United States.
   B. The number of countries in the world keeps increasing.
   C. The cost of travel to some distant countries is very expensive.

Part C SCANNING FOR INFORMATION.　Quickly scan the story to locate the paragraphs in which the following information is given. On a separate piece of paper identify each paragraph by writing the number of the line in which the paragraph begins.

10. Which paragraph tells how old Goddard is now?

11. Which paragraph tells what happened to Goddard's companion on the Congo River expedition?

12. Which paragraph tells that Goddard has flown in a blimp?

13. Which paragraph names some additional adventures he took that were not on his original list?

14. Which paragraph tells how many countries have been added to the world since he created his list?

Part D IDENTIFYING THE SEQUENCE OF EVENTS.　Below are some events from the story. On a separate piece of paper, list the numbers. To the right of the number of the event that occurred first, write "A." To the right of the second one, write "B," etc. Try to answer without referring to the story.

15. Goddard took a Congo River expedition.

16. Goddard made his list.

17. Goddard wrote a book.

18. Goddard rode a horse in the Rose Bowl Parade.

Part E DISCUSSING YOUR REACTIONS AND INSIGHTS.　Consider these questions for possible discussion in the classroom.

19. Which of the adventures and activities mentioned do you personally find most interesting? Why?

20. Do you think that many people "postpone living," as Goddard charges, with excuses such as "not enough time, not enough talent"? Be prepared to justify your answer.

21. What futuristic adventures do you think you will be able to try that Goddard was unable to imagine back in 1940?

Prereading Activities
HOW CELEBRITIES RECALL THEIR FIRST DATES

Part A MAKING PREDICTIONS.   You will be reading a true story that has the title given above.

A "celebrity" is a famous, widely recognized person. Three of the ten celebrities you will be reading about are actresses. Predict other types of celebrities who are probably included in this article by using your hunches about what types of people the general public probably likes to read about.

Part B UNDERSTANDING NEW WORDS.   Below are scrambled definitions of words used in the story you are about to read. Unscramble the definitions by rearranging the phrases. Phrases are separated by double slashes (//). Then write a sentence using each word.

1. **psychologist** (noun) the study of // a person // mental and emotional processes // and their effects on // who specializes in // behavior

2. **confidence** (noun) own abilities // one's // in // belief

3. **tuxedo** (noun) jacket for // tailless // a man's // evening wear

4. **autobiography** (noun) own life // of one's // written by // the story // oneself

Part C FOCUSING YOUR READING.   Now read the story. While you read, decide which celebrity's description of his or her first date you personally find to be most interesting. Be prepared to explain why you find it appealing.

HOW CELEBRITIES RECALL THEIR FIRST DATES

Remember your first date? Some people will never forget theirs. We asked a few celebrities if they recalled what it was like.

Johnny Carson, entertainer: "I was about 8 years old and I was supposed to meet this girl—Peggy Leach was her name—for a movie date in Avoco, Iowa. When I saw her coming I got cold feet and ran away. I guess I didn't want to be seen with a girl and be kidded by the guys. I told that story on the show once and got a letter from her."

Morgan Fairchild, actress: "I was 14 and my date was Felix, a nice, good-looking guy from another school in Dallas. He came over to pick me up and in the meantime, Larry, another guy from my school, was jealous. He came over on the night of the date with his father's shotgun and began cleaning it right in front of poor Felix. I never saw Felix again. Poor Felix."

Dr. Joyce Brothers, psychologist: "I was asked to go out on a date by ... I'm sorry, but I can't remember. I have no brothers, so I had no idea what boys were like. So I went to a library and read every book I could find on how to understand boys and how to get along with them. I was about 11 and it was Laurelton, NY. He came by and off we went to a party. But after reading all those books I felt I could deal with any man. I was full of confidence. I walked home with him, and four other boys came along."

Jane Meadows, actress: "I was about 14 and lived in Sharon, CT. It was a summer date and he was tall, blue-eyed, blond and very handsome—the best-looking boy in the village, I'd say. He could drive a car, so he was about 16. His name was William McLaren Ellison—Mac—and he went to Harvard. He wrote the most beautiful love letters. My first date with him was when we all went over to his house to sing. He would pick me up almost every evening in his car, and he would dust the front seat with a dustcloth. We went together for about two years. The last time I saw him was more than 25 years ago. I had just been divorced and I saw him with his second wife at a train station outside of New York. They looked as if they were arguing. He didn't see me, although we both got on the same train."

Ken Norton, boxer: "My first real car date—I started dating at 11—was my first high-school girlfriend, but I forget her name. It was for the Jacksonville High senior prom in Illinois and I was all decked out in my first tuxedo. I got out to open the car door, and I swooped down into a Prince Valiant bow. The seat of my pants ripped. The worst part was that she heard the split. I thought it might be true love, because we continued on to the dance and my jacket neatly hid the problem."

Phyllis Diller, comedian: "It was a dis-ASTER! I grew a pimple the size of Australia on my nose. And I selected the worst color dress: b-r-o-w-nnnnnn. My date, Charles Crosser, was president of my class and he danced like a kangaroo. It was a dance at Central High School in Lima, Ohio. I was 14 and skinny. I just heard the other day that Crosser is retiring. Well, anyway, he didn't like dancing with me because of my pimple getting in the way. We parked and tried to neck. I felt terrible, but at least it was dark."

Liberace, pianist: "Yes, I remember my first sweetheart very well. She lived in Milwaukee. But I don't care to mention her name, because the last time I mentioned the name of a sweetheart in my autobiography I

was sued for $5 million. Let's just say that my 79
first love was my piano teacher in Milwaukee, 80
Florence Betray Kelly. I was 4 years old." 81

Tanya Roberts, actress: "My first date, at 82
age 13, was with Bryan Leswick at the Pix 83
Theater in the Bronx. I was a complete 84
tomboy and we all went to a Saturday after- 85
noon matinee. The boy placed his arm around 86
me, but because I was a tomboy—and stronger 87
than him—I started beating him up and left 88
the theater, and my date on the floor. He 89
never asked me out again. I think he lives in 90
Canada now." 91

Magic Johnson, basketball player: "Yeah, 92
yeah (laughter). I was in the sixth grade. Her 93
name was Adova Pittman. My father took me 94
to pick her up and then he drove us to see 95
some kind of King Kong monster eat-'em-up 96

movie. We ate popcorn but didn't hold 97
hands. Then after the movie was over, he 98
picked us up again and drove us back to 99
Adova's house. That was in Lansing, Michigan. 100
We went together for the next seven years 101
and we're still good friends. In fact, I'm her 102
best friend and she's my best friend. She's 103
getting married this summer, but not to me." 104

Lucille Ball, entertainer: "My first date? I 105
can't remember his name. Isn't that awful? It 106
was in Celeron Park, NY. I was 16. We went to 107
a Benny Goodman dance at the Pier Ball- 108
room. Six of us. It was wonderful. I went out 109
with him again, too. He became mayor of 110
Jamestown, and yes, I could have seen myself 111
as the wife of the mayor of Jamestown. He 112
was a very, very nice man, I think. 113

"I remember now, his name was Herb 114
Raine. They called him 'Slab.' " 115

Source: John Sherwood, "How Celebrities Recall Their First Dates," Hearst Feature Service, 1982. Reprinted by permission of the publisher.

Postreading Activities
HOW CELEBRITIES RECALL THEIR FIRST DATES:

Part A CHECKING YOUR PREDICTIONS. The answers to Part A of the *Prereading Activities* are entertainer, psychologist, boxer, comedian, pianist, and basketball player.

How many did you correctly predict?

Part B REMEMBERING FACTS. Answer the questions on a separate piece of paper. Try to answer without referring to the story.

1. Which celebrity changed his mind at the last minute and ran away when he saw his first date approaching him?

2. What is the name of the psychologist who described her first date?

3. What did the psychologist do to prepare herself for her first date?

4. What did Jane Meadows and her date do on their first date?

5. What did the celebrity whose pants split on his first date do about the split?

6. What color dress did Phyllis Diller wear on her first date?

7. Why did the celebrity who was a tomboy beat up her first date?

8. Which celebrity says he is still best friends with his first date?

9. Which celebrity had her first date with a man who eventually became a mayor?

Part C DRAWING INFERENCES.   Use everyday reasoning skills to answer the following questions.

10. Johnny Carson mentioned his first date on TV and got a letter from her. Was the letter probably friendly or unfriendly? Why?

11. From the information given by Jane Meadows, infer the age that she must exceed. In other words, she must be older than ....

12. Which celebrity is probably greatly exaggerating the circumstances concerning her first date? Explain your reasoning.

13. Which celebrity has given the name of someone who probably was not his "real" first date? Explain your reasoning.

Part D DISCUSSING YOUR REACTIONS AND INSIGHTS.
Consider these questions for possible discussion in the classroom.

14. Which celebrity's description of his or her first date did you find to be most interesting? Why?

15. Many of the celebrities had their first dates many years ago. As a group, do you think that first dates back then are much different from what they are today? Why?

Prereading Activities
A BOOK TO SWAT ROACHES WITH:
They May Be Brainless, But They're Not Stupid

Part A MAKING PREDICTIONS.   You will be reading a book review with the title given above. Based on that title, predict which of the following is the actual title of the book.

1. Which of the following is probably the title of the book?
    A. The Cockroach: Man's Friend
    B. The Fascinating History of the Cockroach
    C. The Cockroach Combat Manual
    D. The World of Insects

Part B UNDERSTANDING NEW WORDS.   Below are scrambled definitions of words used in the book review you are about to read. Unscramble the definitions by rearranging the phrases. Phrases are separated by double slashes (//). Then write a sentence using each word.

2. **eon** (noun) of time // long period // an indefinitely

3. **fossil** (noun) a remnant or trace // that lived in a past age // of an organism // or a footprint in the earth's crust // such as a skeleton

4. **pesticide** (noun) that is used // any chemical // insects and rodents // to kill

5. **morsel** (noun) or bite // of food // a small piece

6. **initially** (adverb) very // at // beginning // the

7. **implicit** (adjective) understood // implied or // not directly // although // expressed

Part C FOCUSING YOUR READING.   Now read the story. While you read, think about whether humans will ever be able to completely wipe out roaches, even if humans declared an all-out war against them.

A BOOK TO SWAT ROACHES WITH:
They May Be Brainless, But They're Not Stupid

The Cockroach Combat Manual, by Austin M. Frishman and Arthur P. Schwartz, tells us everything we ever wanted to know about the pest—perhaps more than we want to know.

It all began with the Paleoblattidae, ancestors of the modern roach, back in the "Age of Cockroaches," 350 million years ago. The world was young and warm and moist then—and the population of roaches reached its peak. That era ended eons before the dinosaur took its first step.

And in all that time, the cockroach has kept its shape, Frishman says, remaining more or less unchanged, according to the best fossil evidence.

Today, it is able to withstand even drier conditions, reproduce like mad, live in the midst of pesticide and radiation, and go for as long as three weeks without a morsel.

One of the most familiar kitchen cockroaches is *Blattella germanica,* the German cockroach, which can produce as many as 400,000 descendants in a year.

Scientists think they came to Europe from North Africa, carried by Phoenician and Greek trading ships. Some might have migrated directly to the New World on slave ships from Africa or on trading vessels from Europe. No matter. Today, Frishman says, they travel by plane, ship, train and bus. And they are all around us.

Why?

They have resisted every attack from humankind, from the caveman's swatter to the aerosol spray. So it stands to reason that it takes a lot of smarts to survive for 350 million years.

Right? Wrong.

The cockroach has no brains—just a lot of nerve. In fact, what gives the cockroach its scurrying speed are the nerves running directly from its rear-end feelers to its six little legs. But being brainless doesn't mean they're stupid.

Cockroaches can be taught to travel through mazes. They can monitor barometric pressure and take to the high ground before a storm. And before an earthquake, according to the U.S. Geological Survey, they show "marked increase in activity." They sense *something* is going to happen.

With their antennae, they can detect odor and moisture and catch vibrations in the air to sense movement.

So how do you get rid of them?

Frishman has one simple answer: You can't.

"Billions of generations have survived undamaged," he writes, thanks to tremendous reproductive capacity, ability to adapt and protect themselves, and to live on virtually nothing and everything—including paper, soap, toothpaste and, on occasion, toenails.

But do they reflect poor housekeeping?

No, says Frishman. "Initially cockroaches are not prejudiced. They will enter anyone's home. Anyone can get cockroaches; it's only a disgrace to keep them." A population explosion of roaches merely reflects "a sign of indifference."

Frishman suggests that shoppers check all paper 62
bags, cardboard boxes and other packages before 63
bringing them into the house. In apartment houses, he 64
suggests, make sure to plug all holes around pipes 65
with steel wool until they are permanently sealed. 66
Throw out garbage regularly and schedule regular 67
visits by a good pest exterminator. 68

But the future is anything but certain. Pesticides 69
are not the long-range answer, since roaches learn to 70
thrive in a chemical jungle. Only birth control, stifling 71
their reproduction process through chemical formu- 72
lations, offers some hope. 73

Meanwhile, to outwit the roach without the 74
help of an exterminator, Frishman advises, "You 75
need to think like a cockroach." 76

He suggests: Purchase an effective roach insecti- 77
cide. Remove all items from kitchen or bathroom 78
cabinets before spraying. Follow directions and 79
repeat monthly. Be alert to crevices in moist areas— 80
and be ready to call in a professional. 81

The implicit message, of course, is the value of 82
patience. For full satisfaction, you might just have to 83
wait another 350 million years. 84

Source: David Behrens, "A Book to Swat Roaches With, " *Newsday, 1981.* © 1981, Newsday Inc. Reprinted by permission.

Postreading Activities
A BOOK TO SWAT ROACHES WITH:
They May Be Brainless, But They're Not Stupid

Part A CHECKING YOUR PREDICTIONS.   The answer to Part A of the *Prereading Activities* is *The Cockroach Combat Manual.*

Was your prediction correct?

Part B REMEMBERING FACTS.   Answer the questions on a separate piece of paper. Try to answer without looking back at the story.

1. According to the author, did cockroaches or dinosaurs appear first on the earth?

2. Have cockroaches changed their basic shape during the millions of years that they've been on earth?

3. How long can cockroaches live without a bite of food?

4. From what continent did cockroaches first travel to Europe?

5. What do cockroaches do just before a storm?

6. What do cockroaches do just before an earthquake?

7. Name one unusual food cockroaches can live on.

Part C SCANNING FOR INFORMATION.   Quickly scan the story to locate the paragraphs in which the following information is given. On a separate piece of paper, identify each paragraph by writing the number of the line in which the paragraph begins.

8. Which paragraph first mentions the last name of the book's author?

9. Which paragraph tells how many offspring per year the German cockroach can produce?

10. Which paragraph tells how many legs a cockroach has?

11. Which paragraph tells what cockroach's antennae do?

12. Which paragraph states that chemical pesticides are not the long-range solution to getting rid of cockroaches?

Part D DRAWING INFERENCES.   Use everyday reasoning skills to answer the following questions.

13. Why does the author suggest that shoppers check all paper bags (lines 62-63)?

14. Why should all items be removed from kitchen or bathroom cabinets before spraying (lines 78-79)?

15. What does the author probably mean by "full satisfaction" (line 83)?

Part E DISCUSSING YOUR REACTIONS AND INSIGHTS.   Consider these questions for possible discussion in the classroom.

16. Do you think that humans will ever be able to completely wipe out cockroaches? Why?

17. How would you feel and what would you do if you saw a cockroach in your house? In a restaurant?

18. Speculate on the reasons why many people dislike cockroaches.

Prereading Activities
A FORMER BEAUTY QUEEN: 'There's Life After Size 10'

Part A MAKING PREDICTIONS.   You will be reading a true story that has the title given above. Using the information in the title and any hunches you may have, answer each question in a sentence or two.

1. What kind(s) of problems did the former beauty queen probably face?

2. Is the former beauty queen now probably satisfied with herself?

Part B UNDERSTANDING NEW WORDS.   Find the following words in the story in the lines listed below. Do not read the whole story yet, just the paragraph in which each word appears. Try to determine the meanings of the words from the context. List the words on a separate piece of paper and define each.

3. pageant (line 7)
4. launching (line 30)
5. troupe (line 62)

6. audition (line 68)
7. agency (line 94)
8. anonymous (line 97)

Part C FOCUSING YOUR READING.   Now read the entire story. While you read, think about whether it is right and makes sense for advertisers to prefer trim women as models.

A FORMER BEAUTY QUEEN
'There's Life After Size 10'

Irving, TX

A lot has happened to Mary Lou Butler 1
Blaylock since she was named Miss Texas in 2
1965. For one thing, she's gained 50 pounds. 3

"So you can imagine my horror," she 4
says, "when I received an invitation last July 5
to appear at the 25th anniversary celebration 6
of the Miss Texas Pageant. My first reaction 7
was to run and hide. I certainly didn't want to 8
walk out on that stage in my size 18. Not with 9
all those trim little size 6's running around. I 10
went into a fit of depression." 11

But Mary Lou, now 34, says she's always 12
been a fighter, and she's always faced reality. 13
And the reality is that she's no longer a trim 14
17-year-old beauty queen. She's a grown 15
woman who's grown into a large size. 16

"I guess that invitation was my moment 17
of truth," she says. "I could no longer let the 18
fact that I had gained weight ruin my life. I 19
was no longer going to sit around waiting to 20
get thin. I was going to do that show and I was 21
going to look the best I could. I wanted peo- 22
ple to see that there is still life after size 10." 23

She wrote back and told pageant officials 24
she would be there. In accepting, she was 25
required to tell what size T-shirt she wears so 26
she could be fitted for a costume. She re- 27
plied, "Just make sure it's really large." 28

Mary Lou's attitude not only is part of her 29
new philosophy, it's also the launching point 30
for a whole new career. She's come out of the 31
closet, and she doesn't mind telling anyone 32
that the closet contains all size 16's and 18's. 33

"Let's face it," she says. "God made peo- 34
ple in small, medium and large. I'm 5-foot-9. 35
I've put on a lot of weight. I'm what you call 36
large. I just got tired of seeing women with 37
little size 4 bodies modeling clothes that I'm 38
supposed to wear. So I became a model—a 39
large-size model. 40

"I've been fighting weight all my life," 41
she says. "When I was Miss Texas, the pageant 42
people had me working out twice a day. But 43
then it was just a few pounds I was worried 44
about, maybe five or six. I've never been that 45
thin since." 46

She recalls that actress Joan Crawford 47
was a judge in the Miss America Pageant that 48
year. 49

"I didn't win anything in Atlantic City. I 50
wasn't even in the top 10. But when it was all 51
over, Miss Crawford wrote me a letter. She 52
told me I came in No. 11. I was a singer. She 53
said I had a lot of talent and urged me to seek 54
a career. I was very flattered and had been 55
thinking along those lines myself. I had no 56
doubt I was going to be a star." 57

A few days after Mary Lou Butler surren- 58
dered her crown, she was watching television 59
with her family in Irving. Bob Hope was on a 60
program talking about his USO tour. She 61
decided she wanted to be a part of that troupe. 62

"So the next day, I went to the telephone 63
and called Bob Hope in California," she says. 64
"I don't know how I got through to him, but 65
he accepted my call after I identified myself 66
as Miss Texas. I told him about myself and said 67
I wanted to come and audition for him. I said I 68
was bringing my two sisters, Alice Ruth and 69
Nolanda, with me. We were a singing trio." 70

Within a short time, the Butler sisters 71
were in Hollywood. Bob Hope was impressed 72
enough by them to take them on his tour. 73

"We also did a lot of rodeo appearances 74

and things like that," says Mary Lou. "But 75
before long we broke up. One of my sisters 76
got married and we just went our separate 77
ways." 78

Back home in Texas, she worked at 79
various modeling and TV jobs in Dallas. She 80
eventually met Louis Blaylock and settled 81
down to marriage, volunteer work and mother- 82
hood. Her daughter, Alice Andrea, is now 7 83
years old. 84

Mary Lou fit in a few singing engage- 85
ments whenever she could. "Along the way, I 86
just kept putting on weight," she says. "I felt 87
terrible about it. I kept planning my life 88
around losing weight. I wouldn't start any- 89
thing new because I thought I couldn't do it 90
until I'd lost 10 or 20 or 30 pounds. I was very 91
depressed. 92

"Then about a year ago, I went to a model- 93
ing agency with a friend. She had business 94
to conduct. I sat in the corner and tried to 95
ignore all those skinny little bodies walking 96
around. I just wanted to be anonymous." 97

But Kim Dawson, who owns and directs 98
the agency, spied Mary Lou and headed 99
straight for her. 100

"Kim told me she wanted me to start 101
modeling," says Mary Lou. "I told her I'd call 102
her in 40 pounds. She said to stop kidding 103
myself. She said I looked fine just the way I 104
was. 105

"She said the whole world wasn't a size 6 106
and I owed it to all the other large-size 107
women to let them see that someone can be 108
large and still look good." 109

Mary Lou says looking good is important 110
to her. People still see her on the street and 111
point her out as a former Miss Texas. 112

Source: Marlyn Schwartz, "A Former Beauty Queen: There's Life After Size 10," *The Dallas Morning News,* 1981.

Postreading Activities
A FORMER BEAUTY QUEEN: 'THERE'S LIFE AFTER SIZE 10'

Part A CHECKING YOUR PREDICTIONS. These are the answers to Part A of the *Prereading Activities:* 1. Her main problem was keeping her weight down. 2. She is now satisfied with herself.

Which of your predictions were correct?

Part B REMEMBERING FACTS. Answer the questions on a separate piece of paper. Try to answer without looking back at the story.

1. What state did Mary Lou represent when she was a beauty queen?

2. How old is Mary Lou now?

3. What was Mary Lou's reply when asked to tell what size T-shirt she wears?

4. When she was a beauty queen, what specific thing did she do to hold down her weight?

5. What famous person was a beauty queen judge and wrote a letter to Mary Lou?

6. Who took Mary Lou and her sisters on his tour?

7. Why did Mary Lou go to a modeling agency about a year ago?

8. Why do people still point Mary Lou out to each other on the street?

Part C FOLLOWING STRUCTURE.   Answer the following questions on a separate piece of paper. You may go back to the story.

9. What was Mary Lou's last name at the time she was Miss Texas (lines 1 and 58)?

10. To what does "it" (line 28) refer?

11. What is the full name of the "she" (line 53)?

12. To what does "it" (line 88) refer?

13. What is the full name of the "she" (line 104)?

Part D IDENTIFYING THE SEQUENCE OF EVENTS.   Below are some events from the story. On a separate piece of paper, list the numbers. To the right of the number of the event that occurred first, write "A." To the right of the second one, write "B," etc. Try to answer without looking back at the story.

14. Mary Lou called Bob Hope.

15. Mary Lou became Miss Texas.

16. Mary Lou went to a modeling agency.

17. Mary Lou married Louis Blaylock.

18. Mary Lou had a daughter.

Part E DISCUSSING YOUR REACTIONS AND INSIGHTS.   Consider these questions for possible discussion in the classroom.

19. Do you think that it is right and makes sense for advertisers to prefer trim women as models? Why?

20. If you had gained a lot of weight, would it bother you to go to an event such as a class reunion, anniversary celebration, etc., where you would be seen by people who hadn't seen you since you gained the weight? Why?

21. What are some of the other values (in addition to good looks) by which an individual should be judged?

Prereading Activities
FINDING THOSE FASCINATING FACTS

Part A MAKING PREDICTIONS. You will be reading an entertaining newspaper column with the title given above. Predict how the author unearthed his fascinating facts.

Part B UNDERSTANDING NEW WORDS. Determine the meaning of each of the following words by reading the sentences in which they appear. Line numbers are given to help you find the sentences. Do NOT read the entire story yet. Show your understanding by writing, on a separate piece of paper, the letter that gives the best meaning for each.

1. **courier** (line 7)
   A.   a messenger sent with important or urgent messages
   B.   a spicy sauce for beef developed by the French
   C.   an herb used in tomato sauce

2. **fore** (line 18)
   A.   an old, obsolete spelling for "four"
   B.   to be used in place of or instead of
   C.   in or toward the front part of a ship

3. **aft** (line 18)
   A.   at or near the rear of a ship or airplane
   B.   having a special or unusual skill or talent
   C.   dull, dim-witted, or feeble-minded

4. **refugee** (line 19)
   A.   left-over or discarded items of little value
   B.   a person who flees his or her home country to seek safety
   C.   a place where one is secure and safe from harm

5. **virtuoso** (line 29)
   A.   a person with great skill in an art or a science
   B.   a person found guilty of a serious crime
   C.   a person who is crude or vulgar, especially in social situations

6. **predatory** (line 43)
   A.   living a lifestyle characterized by great wealth and fame
   B.   living at the mercy of someone in authority
   C.   living by feeding on other animals

Part C FOCUSING YOUR READING. Now read the entire article. While you read, decide which fact you personally find most fascinating. Be prepared to tell why the one you select is especially fascinating to you.

FINDING THOSE FASCINATING FACTS

Things I learned en route to looking up other things: 1, 2

•That more shipwrecks have been recorded at little-known Sable Island off Nova Scotia than any other place in the Atlantic. At both ends, the island's sandbars run about 17 miles into the ocean. 3, 4, 5, 6

•That in the Middle Ages, the Persian couriers of the Turkish sultans often ran from Constantinople to Adrianople and back, a distance of about 220 miles, in two days and nights (far faster than any horse can run that distance). 7, 8, 9, 10, 11

•That the Rotary Club was so named, at its Chicago founding in 1905, because the first meetings were held in "rotation" at the business offices of various members. 12, 13, 14, 15

•That ancient Greek and Roman vessels were sharp at both ends and could sail either way. There was no "fore" or "aft." 16, 17, 18

•That half the world's refugees are in Africa, although that continent has only 10 percent of the world's population. In the past dozen years its refugee population has increased more than 1,000 percent, owing to political upheaval rather than to natural disasters. 19, 20, 21, 22, 23, 24

•That what is popularly known as "gray matter" of the human brain is really lavender or pink, and is gray only in dead brains. 25, 26, 27

•That composer Franz Liszt, the greatest piano virtuoso of his time, gave up playing the piano in public for the last 40 years of his life. 28, 29, 30

•That pouring hot water into a thin glass is less likely to break it than if poured into a thick glass. (Go ask Isaac Newton why.) 31, 32, 33

•That the term "saint" was originally applied in the New Testament to *all* believers. It was not for 500 years that the word became a title of honor specifically given to the dead whose cult was publicly celebrated in the church. 34, 35, 36, 37, 38

•That the Asian population has more than doubled its size in the U.S. since 1970. It is the fastest-growing racial group in the country. 39, 40, 4

•That there are some 15,000 species of spiders that do *not* spin webs but survive as predatory prowlers. (And of those spiders that do, no two webs are precisely alike.)

•That the door locks on the newest model Rolls-Royces are pin-tumblers patterned after a lock designed in Egypt 4,000 years ago to guard the tomb of a pharoah.

•That in all the developed countries of the world, Belgians have the largest and most spacious homes, averaging 1,800 square feet, followed by American homes, which average 1,500 square feet Russia is at the bottom of the list, averaging unde 600 square feet.

•That the oddly named city in Washington, **56** "Walla Walla," is an Indian term meaning "many **57** waters." **58**

•That until the 19th century, the Congress of the **59** U.S. sat in eight different cities: Philadelphia, Balti- **60** more, Lancaster, York, Princeton, Annapolis, Tren- **61** ton and New York. **62**

•That despite all the "love boat" publicity, the **63** average age of a passenger on a Caribbean cruise ship **64** is 54. **65**

Source: Sydney J. Harris, "Finding Those Fascinating Facts." Reprinted by permission of Sydney J. Harris and Field Newspaper Syndicate, 1982.

Postreading Activities
FINDING THOSE FASCINATING FACTS

Part A CHECKING YOUR PREDICTIONS. The answer to Part A of the *Prereading Activities* is that the author unearthed his fascinating facts while looking up other facts that he needed.

Was your prediction correct?

Part B REMEMBERING FACTS. Answer the following questions by writing "T" for "true" or "F" for "false" on a separate piece of paper. Rewrite each false statement to make it a true statement. Try to answer without looking back at the story.

T F 1. Ancient Greek and Roman ships were the first to have an end designed to be the "fore" and the other designed to be the "aft."

T F 2. Living human brains are gray.

T F 3. Pouring hot water into a thin glass is less likely to break it than if poured into a thick glass.

T F 4. The term "saint" was originally reserved for those who were famous for their good deeds.

T F 5. The fastest-growing racial group in the United States is Caucasian.

T F 6. No two spider webs are exactly alike.

T F 7. Of all developed countries, Russia has the smallest homes.

T F 8. "Walla Walla" is a Scottish term meaning "high mountains."

T F 9. The average age of a passenger on a Caribbean cruise ship is over 50.

Part C DRAWING INFERENCES. Use everyday reasoning skills to answer the following questions with either a "yes" or "no." Be prepared to explain the reasoning you used to reach each answer.

10. Did the author deliberately set out to find the fascinating facts he names?

11. Is it reasonable to infer that Africa is politically stable?

12. Do some people probably incorrectly think that the color of a living brain is gray?

13. Is the author serious about asking Isaac Newton why it's better to pour hot water into thin glasses than thick ones?

14. Is it reasonable to infer from the information given that people in Belgium have better-paying jobs, more and better quality food and clothing, etc. than people in Russia?

Part D DISCUSSING YOUR REACTIONS AND INSIGHTS. Consider these questions for possible discussion in the classroom.

15. Which fact did you personally find most fascinating? Why?

16. Which fact did you personally find the least fascinating? Why?

17. Name a fascinating fact you personally know about other than the ones named in the article. If you don't know one, read the daily newspaper for several days in order to identify one.

Prereading Activities
SURPRISE CHESS CONTENDER: A 15-YEAR-OLD GIRL

Part A MAKING PREDICTIONS.   You will be reading a true story that has the title given above. Most chess contenders are not 15-year-old girls. Using your hunches, predict the age and sex of most chess contenders.

Part B UNDERSTANDING NEW WORDS.   Find the following words in the story in the lines listed below. Do not read the whole story yet, just the paragraph in which each word appears. Try to determine the meanings of the words from context. List the words on a separate piece of paper and define each.

1. veteran (line 15)
2. tournament (line 15)
3. conscious (line 77)
4. arrogance (line 78)
5. accumulate (line 83)
6. circuit (line 85)
7. enduring (line 113)

Part C FOCUSING YOUR READING.   Now read the entire story. While you read, think about what you would personally like and dislike about the type of life this girl leads.

SURPRISE CHESS CONTENDER:
A 15-YEAR-OLD GIRL

Washington, D.C.

Six p.m. in Dupont Circle, a park here; the 1
pawns cast long shadows across the cement tables in 2
the late-afternoon sunlight. Baraka Shabazz, 15 years 3
old and not particularly tall, casts an even longer 4
shadow as she goes from table to table, asking if 5
anyone is interested in a game of chess. 6

It isn't as easy now as it was a few weeks ago, 7
back when she was an unknown, a chubby little black 8
girl in overalls and a green T-shirt, her close-cropped 9
hair concealed under a kerchief, challenging the 10
grown men who play chess in the park. Now she is 11
recognized; she has left a trail of victims. 12

"Baraka?" Paul Glass asks. "Yes, I know 13
Baraka. The little girl who's a candidate master." 14
Glass, a veteran player in Washington tournaments, 15
is a regular visitor to the Dupont Circle tables. He 16
thought he had seen it all until he met Baraka. "I 17
started the first game expecting an easy win," he 18
recalls. "I didn't know what hit me. The second time 19
at least I knew what hit me." 20

It all began a little over three years ago, with 21
cabin fever in Anchorage, Alaska. It was a few days 22
before Christmas in 1977. The Shabazz children, at 23
home on school vacation, were confined indoors by 24
the weather, and their father (who had come to 25
Alaska working on the pipeline) decided he had to do 26
something about it. "He went out and bought us a 27
chess set," Baraka Shabazz recalls, "and he gave it to 28
my sister and me and said, 'Here, play chess.' We told 29
him. 'We don't know how to play,' so he showed us 30
how the pieces work and said, 'You have to get your 31
opponent's king,' and that was the first time I played. 32
Six weeks later, February 6, 1978, I entered my first 33
chess tournament and won three games out of five." 34

Since then the pace has been fast and the 35
direction straight up. She has been invited to play in 36
the U.S. Women's Championship, which is limited to 37
the 12 top-rated players in the country. For a teenager 38
who did not know a rook from a knight four years 39
ago, the accomplishment is amazing. 40

Most of the people she plays in chess tourna- 41
ments are adult white males, and they have trouble 42
taking their opponent seriously when she is a teen- 43
aged black girl. At least until they notice they are 44
losing. Then they have trouble accepting *that* fact. 45

"I have had a lot of opponents blow smoke in 46
my face," she says. "They get red in the face, some of 47
them try to cheat and sometimes they knock the 48
pieces over. A few weeks ago, I had an opponent who 49
was drinking coffee out of a Styrofoam cup. At the 50
beginning he was smiling and relaxed, but then he 51
began nibbling on the cup. By the end of the game, 52
that cup was covered with tooth marks all around the 53
rim. 54

"I remember one tournament where I was 55
playing a 17-year-old boy who came in with his 56
mother. He took one look at me and told her, 'You 57
won't have to wait for me; I'll be back in half an 58
hour.' After he made a couple of moves, he went over 59
to the tournament director. I saw them looking at my 60
name on the list of players—laughing at my name. 61
Well, instead of getting mad, I thought the best way 62
to handle it was to beat him—and to take a long time 63
about it. The game went on for hours, and it kept 64
getting worse for him. Finally I got his queen in a pin; 65
no escape possible. At first, he didn't notice it; he just 66
sat there calmly looking at the board. Then he began 67
to understand the situation, and his face got redder 68
and redder. Finally he just stuck his arm out and 69
swept all the pieces off the table." 70

"It's a real problem," says her mother, Raqiba 71
Shabazz. "We have raised Baraka, like all our chil- 72
dren, to respect her elders, and we have to impress on 73
her that a chess game is a special situation. She has to 74

challenge them, fight them and beat them. But she 75
only does it on the chessboard; it doesn't carry over 76
into life. We are very conscious of the danger of 77
arrogance." 78

"I want to be the best chess player in the world," 79
Baraka says, smiling a little but obviously meaning 80
what she says. Before she can come even close to that, 81
she has a lot of learning to do, a lot of dead-serious 82
games to play, a lot of experience to accumulate. 83

And a lot of money to spend. "We try to follow 84
the tournament circuit," says her mother, "but it gets 85
very expensive. For big tournaments, you can have 86
entry fees of $250 to $300, plus travel tickets and 87
out-of-town living expenses for a week. We're being 88
priced out of the tournament market." 89

Nobody can say yet what her final potential 90
may be, but she is now at about the stage where 91
Bobby Fischer was at age 13, a year before he won 92
the master's title; but by then he had been playing 93
chess more than twice as long as she has. 94

"She may be a genius, but she's still my 15-year- 95
old girl," says Raqiba Shabazz, watching her two 96
youngest children playing on the grass in Dupont 97
Circle. "We try to keep a balance in her life." 98

From the same folder that holds the invitation to 99
the U.S. Championship tournament, Mrs. Shabazz 100
pulls out a 1978 report card. Under "Teacher's 101
Remarks," there are two sentences in a teacher's 102
handwriting: "Thanks for Baraka! Not only is she one 103
of the outstanding 8th-graders, she makes my down 104
times into ups." 105

"We want her to be a young lady as well as a 106
great chess player," says Raqiba Shabazz. "We travel 107
with her and give her good books to read. She wants 108
to learn foreign languages and we would like to give 109
her the opportunity. She puts in long hours at chess 110
and sacrifices a lot. She doesn't have the kind of social 111
life that schoolchildren have; no chance to develop 112
enduring friendships, but we think this talent may be 113
worth the sacrifices." 114

Source: Joseph McLellan, "A Surprise Chess Contender." *The Washington Post,* 1981. Reprinted by permission of the publisher.

Postreading Activities
SURPRISE CHESS CONTENDER: A 15-YEAR-OLD GIRL

Part A CHECKING YOUR PREDICTIONS.   The answer to Part A of the *Prereading Activities* is that most chess contenders are adult males.

Part B REMEMBERING FACTS.   Answer the questions on a separate piece of paper. Try to answer without looking back at the story.

1. In what city is Dupont Circle?

2. In what state did Baraka live when she first played chess?

3. Who first showed Baraka how to play chess?

4. The U.S. Women's Championship games are open only to which players?

5. Why do most people Baraka plays have trouble taking her seriously at first?

6. What did the 17-year-old boy that Baraka describes do after he realized that he could not win the game?

7. Baraka's mother wants her to challenge and fight adults only under one circumstance. What circumstance?

8. About how much are the entry fees for a big tournament?

9. What else has Baraka specifically said she would like to learn?

Part C *IDENTIFYING THE SEQUENCE OF EVENTS.*   Below are some events from the story. On a separate piece of paper, list the numbers. To the right of the number of the event that occurred first, write "A." To the right of the second one, write "B," etc. Try to answer without referring to the story.

10. Baraka was invited to play in the U.S. Women's Championship.

11. Baraka first learned how to play chess.

12. Baraka's family moved to Alaska.

13. Baraka plays in her first tournament.

14. A reporter interviewed Baraka's mother for information for the story that you have just read.

Part D *IDENTIFYING MAIN IDEAS.*   Answer each question by selecting the best choice. You may go back to the story.

15. Which of the following best expresses the main idea of the paragraph that begins on line 13?
    A. Paul Glass is a veteran player in Washington tournaments.
    B. A veteran player was surprised at Baraka's skill when he first played against her.
    C. Baraka is so highly skilled at playing chess that she's become a candidate master.

16. Which of the following best expresses the main idea of the paragraph that begins on line 35?
    A. Baraka has made amazing accomplishments in the world of chess in just four years.
    B. The U.S. Women's Championship is limited to the 12 top-rated players in the country.
    C. Four years ago, Baraka did not know the difference between a rook and knight.

17. Which of the following best expresses the main idea of the paragraph that begins on line 71?

    A. Baraka's mother thinks that Baraka is such a genius that adults could learn a lot of different things from Baraka.

    B. Baraka's mother tries to teach Baraka the same types of values that she teaches her other children.

    C. Baraka's mother wants Baraka to respect her elders even though Baraka can beat some adults at chess.

18. Which of the following best expresses the main idea of the paragraph that begins on line 84?

    A. The entry fee for a big tournament can range up to $300.

    B. Having Baraka play in tournaments puts a financial strain on her family.

    C. Travel tickets and out-of-town living expenses have to be paid by Baraka's family.

Part E DISCUSSING YOUR REACTIONS AND INSIGHTS. Consider these questions for possible discussion in the classroom.

19. What would you personally like and dislike about the type of life that Baraka leads? Why?

20. How would you personally feel and how would you react if you were Baraka and an opponent blew smoke in your face?

21. Speculate on some of the reasons why Baraka's family is willing to spend a lot of money so that Baraka can play chess in tournaments.

Prereading Activities
THE LITTLE CAT THAT COULD

Part A MAKING PREDICTIONS.   You will be reading a true story that has the title given above. The cat was turned in to the animal shelter when she was a kitten because she "acted odd." Use your hunches to predict what was so odd about her that her owners gave her to the shelter.

Part B UNDERSTANDING NEW WORDS.   Find the following words in the story in the lines listed below. Do not read the entire story yet, just the paragraph in which each word appears. Try to determine the meanings of the words from the context. List the words on a separate piece of paper and define each.

1. feline (line 11)
2. foster (line 23)
3. rehabilitate (line 29)
4. predicament (line 73)

5. accommodate (line 81)
6. compensate (lines 94-95)
7. impairments (line 95)
8. anecdotes (line 114)

Part C FOCUSING YOUR READING.   Now read the entire story. While you read, think about whether you would want the cat described in the story as your own pet. Why?

THE LITTLE CAT THAT COULD

San Francisco, CA

The tiny ball of fur lay silently on the Shelter 1
counter. At eight weeks old, she was the only 2
kitten that "acts odd," her owners explained. 3
They knew there was something wrong with the 4
animal, but with the mother and other kittens to 5
worry about, the time and money for extensive 6
care was unavailable. So she was given up at the 7
San Francisco SPCA.* 8

Members of the Shelter staff and a con- 9
cerned volunteer gathered round, hoping to find 10
out what was so different about the little feline. 11
She was very quiet. She looked healthy and 12
purred happily when touched or held, but her 13
responses to sound and moving objects were 14
more than just slow—they were almost non- 15
existent. Examinations and tests by SF/SPCA 16
veterinarians revealed the source of the problem: 17
the pretty brown and black tiger cat was deaf 18
and blind. 19

With such serious disabilities, she might be 20
difficult to place. No one could be certain if the 21
kitten would ever adapt and adjust—even under 22
the best of circumstances. She needed a foster 23
parent, a person with lots of patience and love. 24
Through the SF/SPCA's Foster Care Program, 25
volunteers, staff and other friends of the animals 26
provide temporary refuge for Shelter guests 27
needing extra help. This special care helps to 28
rehabilitate animals recovering from surgery or 29
undergoing medical treatment, and aids the 30
young ones until they mature to an age where 31
they can be placed in good, new homes. In the 32
case of the deaf, blind feline, a temporary home 33
was needed to determine whether the kitten 34
could survive as a pet in a household environ- 35
ment. Although she couldn't foster the little cat 36
herself, Dixie Tracy-Kinney, an SF/SPCA Volun- 37

teer, was determined to find someone who 38
could. 39

"There was something about her," Dixie 40
replies, when asked why she was drawn to this 41
particular kitten. "She was so innocent and 42
trusting." Working desperately to find a foster 43
home for "Helen Keller," as the cat was now 44
being called, Dixie posted flyers describing the 45
handicapped feline all over the Pacific Telephone 46
building where she worked. At first, much of the 47
response was negative. "Everyone laughed at 48
me—they told me I was crazy," she remembers. 49
But Maggie Sutton's reaction to the flyer was 50
different. A long-time animal lover, she was 51
touched by Helen's story and wanted to help. 52
Maggie agreed to act as a temporary parent, to 53
see if Helen could adapt to life without vision or 54
hearing. 55

"She was very helpless at first," Maggie 56
recalls. "But after she became used to the 57
house, you'd swear she wasn't blind." Helen 58
was doing beautifully in her foster home, but 59
before she was six months old, Maggie and her 60
husband were forced to move to a house where 61
pets were not allowed. The little deaf, blind 62
feline would have to be given up again. Maggie 63
couldn't bear the thought of losing Helen, and 64
asked her mother-in-law to take the little cat. 65
Helen had proven that she could adjust to a 66
regular home life, Maggie believed. All she 67
needed now was a permanent place to do it in. 68

With four felines, a dog and a dove already 69
in residence, the last thing Diana Sutton was 70
looking for was another pet. But Helen's won- 71
derful disposition and interesting personality, com- 72
bined with her physical predicament, won Diana 73
over, convincing her that one more animal in the 74

* Society for the Prevention of Cruelty to Animals.

household really wouldn't be much of a prob- 75
lem. "We knew that she really needed looking 76
out for," Diana says. "But we were also con- 77
fident that Helen could eventually be just like 78
any other pet." 79

The Suttons made only a few adjustments 80
to accommodate the new addition to their 81
family. Plastic sheeting was put in to guard the 82
open areas around the stairway, just in case of a 83
wrong step. Instead of string or commercial cat 84
toys, Diana came up with the idea of using small 85
onions and potatoes, the perfect playthings to 86
entice the little cat's senses. Helen also de- 87
veloped a love for glazed donuts. Drawn only by 88
the smell, she can detect the presence of dinner, 89
donuts or other delectable treats no matter 90
where she is in the house. "I don't know how she 91
does it, but when food's around, she's right 92
there," Diana reports. Helen's senses of smell 93
and touch have gradually strengthened to com- 94
pensate for her vision and hearing impairments. 95
She follows the other cats by their scent and has 96
become as well-adjusted as the rest of her 97
seeing, hearing family. 98

Today, visitors to the Sutton home can 99
rarely tell which of their cats is deaf and blind. 100
"She's always the center of attention because, 101
when people find out, they can't believe it," 102
Diana says. Helen is now called "The Kitten" by 103
Diana and her husband. The little cat gets along 104
fine with the four other feline members of her 105
family. Her favorite, though, is "Sammy," a male 106
Siamese mix that "moved in" with the Suttons 107
after regularly eating meals at their doorstep. 108
The two are often found washing each other or 109
cuddled up on the couch, asleep. 110

Interested in The Kitten's progress and 111
activities, Dixie inquires periodically to see how 112
the cat is doing. The three women share pic- 113
tures, anecdotes and warm feelings for the 114
fortunate little feline—a cat that, with faith, patience 115
and help from very special people, defied her 116
physical disabilities and now leads what appears 117
to be a normal, if somewhat pampered, life. 118

From sensitive, compassionate people to a 119
remarkable little animal, the circle is complete. 120
This formerly helpless kitten has learned—and 121
goes on teaching—the real meaning of love. 122

Source: "The Little Cat That Could," *Our Animals*, San Francisco Society for the Prevention of Cruelty to Animals, 1982. Reprinted by permission of the publisher.

Postreading Activities
THE LITTLE CAT THAT COULD

Part A CHECKING YOUR PREDICTIONS. The answer to the question posed in Part A of the *Prereading Activities* is that the little cat was deaf and blind.

Was your prediction correct?

Part B REMEMBERING FACTS. Answer the questions on a separate piece of paper. Try to answer without looking back at the story.

1. How old was the kitten when she was brought to the animal shelter?

2. In what city was the shelter located?

3. What is the purpose of the Foster Care Program?

4. Why did the cat's first foster parents have to give her up?

5. What types of "toys" were given to the cat?

6. Can visitors usually tell that the cat is deaf and blind?

7. What two names were given to the cat?

Part C SCANNING FOR INFORMATION. Quickly scan the story to locate the paragraphs in which the following information is given. Identify each paragraph by writing the number of the line in which the paragraph begins on a separate piece of paper.

8. Which paragraph says that the cat was examined by veterinarians?

9. Which paragraph first mentions that the cat was deaf and blind?

10. Which paragraph says that the cat was called "Helen Keller"?

11. Which paragraph says that the cat enjoyed donuts?

12. Which paragraph says that the cat often slept cuddled up with another cat?

Part D DRAWING INFERENCES. Use everyday reasoning skills to answer the following questions with either a "yes" or "no." Be prepared to explain the reasoning you used to reach each answer.

13. Do most people prefer to have a pet that can take care of itself?

14. Does the SPCA regularly get animals that need special care and attention?

15. Is the cat in this story likely to end up back in the SPCA?

Part E DISCUSSING YOUR REACTIONS AND INSIGHTS. Consider these questions for possible discussion in the classroom.

16. Would you want to be the owner of the cat described in this story? Why?

17. Since many pets without handicaps are homeless, is it fair for the SPCA to use resources to help handicapped pets if this means that there will be fewer resources for nonhandicapped but homeless pets? Why?

Prereading Activities
THE SWEET ART OF JELLYBEAN MOSAICS

Part A MAKING PREDICTIONS.   You will be reading a story that has the title given above. A *mosaic* is "a picture or design made by putting together small pieces of colored stone, glass, or other material." The central character makes mosaics using jellybeans. Predict some of the types of pictures he makes. (*Hint:* A famous person is very fond of jellybeans.)

Part B UNDERSTANDING NEW WORDS.   Determine the meaning of each of the following words by reading the sentences in which they appear. Line numbers are given to help you find the sentences. Do NOT read the entire story yet. Show your understanding by writing, on a separate piece of paper, the letter that gives the best meaning for each.

1. **graphics** (line 4)

    A.   the art of making drawings following mathematical rules
    B.   colored pens used by illustrators and other artists
    C.   a special type of camera used to duplicate works of art

2. **predilection** (line 11)

    A.   a premonition that something undesirable will happen
    B.   a partiality or preference for something
    C.   the ability to predict future events

3. **muse** (line 18)

    A.   to think deeply and at length
    B.   to make fun of or to laugh at
    C.   someone who is recognized as a great musical composer

4. **adorn** (line 73)

    A.   to worship and respect
    B.   to put decorations on, to decorate with
    C.   to hold together temporarily

5. **caricature** (line 73)

    A.   a chocolate candy with a liquid, fruit-flavored filling
    B.   the storage space in a vehicle such as a car or truck
    C.   a drawing or representation of a person with certain features exaggerated

6. **perplexed** (line 88)

    A.   full of doubt or uncertainty, puzzled
    B.   extremely happy, joyful
    C.   very eager or willing, submissive

7. **logo** (line 96, short for "logotype")

    A. a typesetting machine that puts type into narrow columns
    B. a type of person who has limited verbal abilities
    C. a distinctive trademark, often used by a company

8. **hue** (line 104)

    A. a difficult concept or position
    B. oversized or larger than normal
    C. a particular shade or tint of color

9. **barometer** (line 132)

    A. a measuring cup marked with metric units
    B. a licensed place for serving alcoholic beverages
    C. anything that reflects or indicates change or reactions

Part C FOCUSING YOUR READING. Now read the entire story. While you read, think about whether you personally believe that art made with jellybeans is "real art."

THE SWEET ART OF JELLYBEAN MOSAICS

San Francisco, CA

Peter Rocha can boast that he's king of the "sweet arts." 1 2

Jellybean art, that is. 3

Rocha, 44, is a San Francisco graphics designer and illustrator. He creates pieces of mosaic art—be they portraits, cowboy boots, hats, plaques, Valentines, whatever—out of hundreds and thousands of jellybeans. 4 5 6 7 8

The idea of using sugar-coated candies in art work stemmed from President Reagan's much publicized predilection for jellybeans. 9 10 11

In fact, his first piece of jellybean art work was a full-sized portrait of the President. The four-foot by four-foot caricature contains 9,000 jellybeans! That was followed by a portrait of Reagan, wife Nancy and the ex-actor's horse. "It looked like a picture of Roy Rogers, Dale Evans and Trigger," mused Rocha. 12 13 14 15 16 17 18 19

The media and general public responded like ants to, well ... jellybeans. Rocha suddenly appeared on local and national television programs. There was coverage in major magazines. And there were the radio shows. He had created a monster. Jellybean art was formed! 20 21 22 23 24 25 26

"I told myself I was going to go with the event—with whatever was happening." 27 28

Rocha's next jellybean project came after the San Francisco 49ers won the Super Bowl last year. The hoopla and hysteria he observed in the city following the Niners' victory over Cincinnati prompted him to do a jellybean portrait of the Super Bowl's quarterback Joe Montana. 29 30 31 32 33 34 35

Quite a different type of clash inspired his next jellybean dream. The Falklands. Great Britain vs. Argentina. A portrait of Britain's Prime Minister Margaret Thatcher, of course. 36 37 38 39

Portraits of Elvis Presley and Burt Reynolds followed. Then a portrait of the Pope. 40 41

He created one of Queen Elizabeth II in time for her recent visit to San Francisco. Rocha even tried to hand-deliver the portrait to Her Majesty herself. 42 43 44 45

"I had some problems with security," he said, trying to conceal a laugh and delivering perhaps the classic of understatements. "But it was a big hit with the media. Actually, the story came out that I got kicked out the St. Francis Hotel (where the queen was staying in San Francisco), which wasn't true but it made a good story."

There was even TV footage of the portrait being loaded aboard the Britannia. And the BBC wanted copies of the footage so it could be shown in England.

"People felt that if anywhere they'd find something as absurd as jellybean art, it would be in San Francisco."

"Real People," "You Asked for It," "Claim to Fame" (Canadian television's version of "What's My Line?," created by the same producers, Mark Goodson and Bill Toddman) didn't have much trouble finding Rocha and encouraging him to appear on their programs. He was highlighted in Herb Caen's *San Francisco Chronicle* column. Then there were *Time* magazine and other major publications. *National Geographic,* too. Even the cover of the February 1983 edition of Sesame Street Magazine, *The Electric Company,* was adorned in a jellybean caricature of the famed Spiderman. Disneyland has also expressed interest in his works.

Soon he will appear on Channel 5's "Pacific Currents." For those of you who will be in Southern California Easter Sunday, he'll be featured in an Easter special on KNXT television, Burbank.

"It's all been a blur," observed the native of San Antonio, Texas, trying to describe the jellybean fuss.

Rocha at one time had accumulated between 600 and 700 pounds of jellybeans, an investment that has made the people at Herman Goelitz's jellybean factory in Oakland very happy, if not somewhat perplexed. Jellybean art has not completely taken over his business ("It's a fluctuating thing," he notes), but it has certainly proven to be a major distraction.

He says that in order to survive financially, he still must rely on and stick with his graphic arts and illustration business, designing logos and labels for businesses such as restaurants and stereo stores, designing stationery, record album covers, movie posters, and packaging labels. But the specter of jellybean art persists.

"At first I tried using tweezers to put the jellybeans on one at a time. Soon, I asked myself, 'How do I get out of this?' "

There are 20 different hues and 36 different flavors of jellybeans. Working from a pile of several hundred jellybeans, Rocha has mastered the technique by utilizing chopsticks in manipulating the pieces of mosaic jellybean art. And besides, he never goes hungry.

The jellybean mosaics—be they the more routine works of plaques, Valentines, birthday greetings and the like, or the occasional portrait—take three to four days to cure, he said.

Never having created any type of mosaic art before, Rocha, who has had some formal art schooling in New York, consulted Roman and Greek art books, mastering the "corn row effect," as he calls it. Whereas the first portrait of Reagan took him about three weeks to finish, he can generally polish off a jellybean project in about a week's time now.

But the true satisfaction he gets out of jellybean art is the reactions from people— particularly children—when they first catch sight of one of his works. "It's the double-take when people first see it," he observes. "They question the texture. Then they discover the jellybeans. Then they repeat the whole process."

The "real barometer" for jellybean art is the reaction from children, Rocha admits. "By far, they're the most spontaneous. Their response is always the most honest ... always right on the surface."

"It's not the real world. Jellybean art is so hard ... to fit in. It breaks the standard. Frankly, I don't know what to do with it myself."

The future of jellybean art is uncertain. 141
Rocha already likens himself to a "mad scien- 142
tist in his lab, somebody who doesn't fit the 143
mold." He says that he hasn't really prepared 144
any jellybean art for Easter this year but is 145
looking forward to coming up with some- 146
thing for next Easter. "Eddie Rabbit, maybe?" 147
he asks himself. 148

He was due to work up a portrait of a 149
well-known Japanese actor ("who looks like 150
James Dean," he laughed) last week. And 151
who knows what lies ahead? 152

There is the family—his wife, Jane Lynch 153
Rocha, a native of Ireland, and two sons, 154
Peter Ireland, 15, and Romero Shannon, 13. 155
There are the requests for speaking and 156
media engagements for which he has little 157
time anymore. There's his art and illustration 158
business. 160

And enough jellybeans to last a lifetime. 161
"It defies me completely." 162

Source: John Lynch, "The Sweet Art of Jellybean Mosaics," *The Sonoma Index-Tribune,* 1983. Reprinted by permission of the publisher.

Postreading Activities
THE SWEET ART OF JELLYBEAN MOSAICS

Part A CHECKING YOUR PREDICTIONS. The answer to Part A of the *Prereading Activities* is that the central character makes portraits—especially of famous people such as President Reagan—plaques, Valentines, and birthday greetings.

Was your prediction on the right track?

Part B REMEMBERING FACTS. Answer the following questions by writing "T" for "true" or "F" for "false" on a separate piece of paper. Rewrite each false statement to make it a true statement. Try to answer without looking back at the story.

T F 1. The central character, Peter Rocha, lives in Washington, D.C.

T F 2. Rocha got the idea for jellybean art from President Reagan's liking for jellybeans.

T F 3. Up to this point, the news media has ignored Rocha's jellybean art.

T F 4. Rocha has done a portrait of Elvis Presley.

T F 5. Rocha has done a portrait of Queen Elizabeth II.

T F 6. Rocha is a native of San Francisco.

T F 7. Rocha earns his entire income from his jellybean art.

T F 8. It now takes Rocha about three weeks to do a jellybean art project.

Part C IDENTIFYING MAIN IDEAS. On a separate piece of paper, state the main idea of each of the following paragraphs. Use only one complete sentence to state each main idea.

9. the paragraph that begins on line 61

10. the paragraph that begins on line 93

11. the paragraph that begins on line 141

Part D INTERPRETING FIGURES OF SPEECH. On a separate piece of paper, explain in your own words the literal (actual) meaning of each of the following phrases.

12. "responded like ants to" (lines 20-21)

13. "had created a monster" (line 25)

14. "it's all been a blur" (line 81)

15. "polish off" (line 122)

16. "somebody who doesn't fit the mold" (lines 143-144)

Part E DISCUSSING YOUR REACTIONS AND INSIGHTS. Consider these questions for possible discussion in the classroom.

17. Do you personally think that the art made with jellybeans is "real art"?

18. Do you think that children (see lines 132-136) are the best judges or barometers for art in general? Why? For jellybean art? Why?

19. Who or what would you like to see done in jellybean art? Why?

Prereading Activities
ECHO: A VICTIM OF ANIMAL ABUSE

Part A MAKING PREDICTIONS.   You will be reading a story that has the title given
above. "Echo" is the name of a dog. There are many ways in which a
dog may be abused. Name two ways that you think might be mentioned
in the story. While you read, check to see if the ways you've named are
ones mentioned in the story.

Part B UNDERSTANDING NEW WORDS.   Find the following words in the story in
the lines listed below. Do not read the entire story yet, just the paragraph
in which each word appears. Try to determine the meanings of the
words from the context. List the words on a separate piece of paper and
define each.

1. nurtured (line 8)
2. resilient (line 15)
3. incarcerated (line 22)
4. custody (line 53)

5. beneficiary (line 59)
6. canine (line 91)
7. infirmary (line 105)
8. resounding (line 110)

Part C FOCUSING YOUR READING.   Now read the entire story. While you read,
think about whether you personally think the dog's original owner should
have been punished.

ECHO: A Victim of Animal Abuse

San Francisco, CA

Cruelty to animals is an ugly crime. The 1
victims cannot call for help and can't testify 2
about their pain. Some of them die while 3
being abused. Some are suffering so much 4
when they are found, their lives cannot be 5
saved. But, thanks to people who care to get 6
involved, others are rescued in time to be 7
treated and nurtured back to health. These 8
can be placed in new, good homes, where 9
they learn to trust people again. 10

This is the story of Echo, a two-year-old 11
terrier mix that knew little but mistreatment 12
from human hands before she reached the 13
San Francisco SPCA.* For this remarkably 14
resilient little dog, a life of pain and misery 15
has become a new life filled with service and 16
love. 17

*Society for the Prevention of Cruelty to Animals.

Echo first came to our attention when 18
the Police Department arrested her owner 19
for a traffic violation. The SF/SPCA routinely 20
gives refuge to animals whose owners are 21
incarcerated until arrangements can be made 22
for their release. The dog was examined on 23
arrival at our Shelter and found to be in need 24
of some attention. The SF/SPCA veterinarian 25
discovered evidence of a skin problem and 26
thought she looked a little thin. Echo was fed 27
and treated before being kenneled for the 28
night. 29

When her owner came to claim her the 30
next day, the dog's potential problems were 31
discussed with him in detail. He assured the 32
Shelter staff that Echo had been seeing a veter- 33
inarian and was scheduled for another ap- 34
pointment very soon. The dog was released 35
to him on the condition that he take her for 36
additional medical treatment before the skin 37
problem grew any worse, and that he follow 38
his veterinarian's advice regarding proper 39
nutrition for the animal. The owner seemed 40
genuinely concerned about his pet. He 41
promised to see to Echo's needs right away. 42

Three weeks later, the Shelter received a 43
report that a dog had been left tied to a park- 44
ing meter on a busy street. It had been there a 45
long time, the caller said. When the SF/SPCA 46
Officer arrived at the scene, she saw with 47
horror that it was Echo. The animal's condi- 48
tion had deteriorated dramatically. She looked 49
malnourished and was almost hairless. There 50
were open sores all over her body. 51

This time, Echo was taken into protective 52
custody by the San Francisco SPCA. This time, 53
she would not be returned to her owner 54
under any condition. This time, he was found, 55
cited for cruelty to animals, prosecuted and 56
punished for his crime. 57

At the SF/SPCA Infirmary, Echo became 58
the beneficiary of our Cinderella Fund—a 59
special program which provides help to Shel- 60
ter animals needing extensive care and atten- 61
tion, begun several years ago by kind con- 62
tributors to the Society. She was placed on a 63
special diet and began receiving regular treat- 64
ments to heal her wounds and cure her skin 65
condition. Because she would need medical 66
care over a long period of time, our SF/SPCA 67
Humane Officer gave the dog a foster home 68
where she could live comfortably until she 69
was healthy again. 70

Despite her ordeal at the hands of her 71
former owner, Echo quickly learned to trust 72
the human beings who were handling her so 73
gently. She responded well to treatment and 74
grew sturdy on a high-nutrition diet. Her skin 75
began to heal and was gradually covered by a 76
new, healthy coat. Her foster parent found 77
her to be exceptionally intelligent and alert. 78
She suggested that Echo be tested for the 79
Society's Hearing Dog Program—and the 80
little dog passed with flying colors. 81

"She's a natural!" her trainers exclaimed 82
as a happy, frisky Echo sailed through her 83
four months of intensive training as an SF/ 84
SPCA Hearing Dog. She went about her work 85
with enthusiasm and excitement. Her re- 86
sponses were consistent and reliable. She 87
seemed to thrive on human contact and was 88
eager to please her new friends. 89

The Training Center staff had been 90
screening canine candidates for months, seek- 91
ing another dog to help demonstrate the 92
program. Hearing Dogs must be bright, depend- 93
able and responsive, so their deaf guardians 94
can be sure they will be alerted every time 95
specific signals sound. "Demonstration Hear- 96
ing Dogs" must be all that and more—able to 97
show exactly how the training works without 98
being distracted by strange surroundings, the 99
presence of an audience, stage lights, camer- 100
as or microphones. They must be extraordi- 101
nary animals. And Echo filled the bill. 102

From a victim of abuse and the subject of 103
a cruelty investigation, through special care 104
at our Shelter and Infirmary, with the help of 105
our Foster Care Program and Cinderella 106
Fund, Echo has become a star and a symbol of 107
the San Francisco's SPCA Hearing Dog Pro- 108
gram. Her name suits her perfectly—not just 109
because she's a resounding success as a Hear- 110
ing Dog, but because this courageous little 111
canine has literally "bounced back" to a 112
brand new life. 113

Source: "Echo," *Our Animals,* San Francisco Society for the Prevention of Cruelty to Animals, 1982. Reprinted by permission of the publisher.

Postreading Activities
ECHO: A VICTIM OF ANIMAL ABUSE

Part A CHECKING YOUR PREDICTIONS. The answer to the question posed in Part A of the *Prereading Activities* was that the dog was given neither proper nutrition nor proper medical attention for its ailment.

Part B REMEMBERING FACTS. Answer the questions on a separate piece of paper. Try to answer without looking back at the story.

1. In what city did the events occur?

2. Why was Echo first taken to the SPCA?

3. Was the dog's original owner a man or a woman?

4. Why did Echo come the SPCA's attention the second time?

5. What is the name of the fund that provides help to Shelter animals needing extensive care and attention?

6. Echo received special training for what kind of job?

Part C FOLLOWING STRUCTURE. Answer the following questions on a separate piece of paper. You may go back to the story.

7. To whom does "them" (line 3) refer?

8. To what does "these" (line 8) refer?

9. What is the name of the "dog" mentioned in line 15?

10. Who is "him" (line 32)?

11. Who is "he" (line 55)?

12. Who is "she" (line 66)?

13. Who is "she" (line 79)?

14. Who are "they" (line 101)?

15. What is the name of the "canine" (line 112)?

Part D IDENTIFYING THE AUTHOR'S TONE. Write the number of the following items on a separate piece of paper. Identify how you think the author feels about each by writing "good" or "bad" for each. Use the context of the story to identify the answers.

16. The SF/SPCA veterinarian.

17. Echo's original owner.

18. The Cinderella Fund

19. The judge who sentenced Echo's original owner.

20. The Hearing Dog Program

Part E DISCUSSING YOUR REACTIONS AND INSIGHTS. Consider these questions for possible discussion.

21. Is it possible that Echo's original owner thought that he wasn't "really" doing anything wrong? Explain.

22. Is it possible to justify giving money to the Cinderella Fund for animals instead of giving money to funds that feed starving children in other parts of the world? Explain.

Prereading Activities
GAINS AND LOSSES FOR AMERICAN WOMEN:

Part A *MAKING PREDICTIONS.* You will be reading a true story that has the title given above. It was written in 1982. Try to think of a particular achievement made by a woman at about that time that might be mentioned in the article.

Part B *UNDERSTANDING NEW WORDS.* Below are words used in the story you are about to read. List them on a separate piece of paper. To the right of each word, write its meaning, selecting from the scrambled list.

Word	*Meaning (listed in scrambled order)*
1. ratification	A. to lead a drive or attack
2. remobilize	B. to prepare or put into action again
3. tactic	C. a high-level assistant
4. spearhead	D. something just and fair
5. flex	E. to bend or contract, as a muscle
6. correspondent	F. one who writes from a distance for newspapers, magazines, etc.
7. aeronautics	G. the act of officially confirming or approving something
8. equity	H. a maneuver or means for achieving a goal
9. deputy	I. the science of aircraft construction and navigation

Complete each of the following sentences by substituting one of the preceding words for the blank. The sentences are not part of the story but are given to help you understand the new words. (Do NOT write on this page. Rewrite the sentences on a separate piece of paper.)

10. After we lost the battle, we had to _____ our troops before the next attack.

11. Because she is well known in the community, we will ask her to _____ our fund-raising drive.

12. Her _____ took over her duties while she was on vacation.

13. The civil rights leader said his group did not want special privileges, just _____ .

14. Our _____ sent us the story by mail.

15. We decided to _____ our muscles and call a red alert.

16. _____ of this amendment will require only a majority to vote in its favor.

17. Because of her interest in _____ , she applied for a job with the Air Force.

18. In the next battle, we decided to try a new _____ .

Part C FOCUSING YOUR READING.   Now read the story. Mentioned are numerous achievements of specific women. While you read, think about which achievement you think was most important and why.

GAINS AND LOSSES FOR AMERICAN WOMEN

Editor's Note: The following article was prepared in 1982. It is presented here to help the reader put current issues regarding women's rights into historical perspective.

NEW YORK

The ERA is dead. Long live the ERA! 1

That was the reaction of supporters of 2 the Equal Rights Amendment, a measure that 3 was reintroduced in the U.S. Senate and 4 House of Representatives just 14 days after 5 the June 30, 1982, ratification deadline passed. 6

The original amendment died because 7 only 35 of the 38 states required to make it 8 part of the Constitution had ratified the mea- 9 sure. The end came 10 years after it was 10 approved by Congress in 1972 and after the 11 seven-year ratification limit was extended by 12 three years in 1979. 13

But as opponents celebrated their vic- 14 tory when time ran out, proponents vowed to 15 remobilize with a new tactic: to turn the anti- 16 ERA politicians out of office and to elect 17 more women to seats in the state legislatures. 18

Eleanor Smeal, president of the National 19 Organization for Women, which spearheaded 20 the last-ditch ERA Countdown Campaign, 21 declared that women had just begun to flex 22 their political muscles. 23

NOW, which was involved in several 24 hundred national and state races last No- 25 vember, said that of the 109 NOW-supported 26 candidates at the congressional level, 61 per- 27 cent had been elected. 28

There are now 21 congresswomen, com- 29 pared with 20 women in Congress in 1980. 30

Women made significant gains in other 31 fields in 1982: 32

President Reagan installed Vivian Vahl- 33 berg, Washington correspondent for the *Daily* 34 *Oklahoman*, as the first woman president of 35 the National Press Club. "After 74 years, it's 36 about time!" Reagan said. 37

The National Aeronautics and Space Ad- 38 ministration announced that Dr. Sally K. Ride, 39 31, an astrophysicist, will become the first 40 American woman to fly in space. She is sched- 41 uled to go on the seventh space shuttle mis- 42 sion, slated for early 1983. 43

Lt. Mary Jane Wixom took command of 44 the Coast Guard cutter Cape Strait, the first 45 female graduate of the Coast Guard Academy 46 to be given command of a cutter. Her crew 47 consists of 12 men. 48

Columbia College (not the university), 49 the last all-male college in the Ivy League, an- 50 nounced that the 228-year-old school will 51 admit women students in the autumn of 1983. 52

At Harvard, another Ivy League school, 53 Lisa Henson, 22, was elected president of the 54 nation's oldest college humor magazine. She 55 is the first woman to head *The Harvard Lam-* 56 *poon* in its 106 years of existence. 57

And at Yale, Andee Hochman became 58 the second woman in its 105-year history to 59 be elected editor-in-chief of the *Yale Daily* 60 *News*. 61

For the first time in its 69 years, Actors 62 Equity Association has a woman as its presi- 63 dent. Ellen Burstyn, 49, Oscar and Tony winner, 64 is the top officer of the 30,000-member union. 65

Dr. Suzanne Knoebel, 55, became the 66 first woman to head the American College of 67 Cardiology, an organization of heart special- 68 ists. Dr. Faye Abdellah, who received a doctor- 69 ate in educational psychology from Colum- 70 bia University, has become the first woman 71 and the first nurse in the 184-year history of 72 the Public Health Service to be named dep- 73 uty surgeon general. 74

Sculptor Charlotte Dunwiddie was unani- 75 mously selected by her peers as president of 76 the National Sculpture Society, the first woman 77

to head the group since its founding in 1893. 78

Sherma E. Bierhaus, 46, is the first woman 79 to be put in charge of a national park. A 80 19-year veteran of the National Park Service, 81 she was appointed unit manager of the Arches 82 National Park near Moab, Utah. Bierhaus was 83 born in Arizona's Grand Canyon National 84 Park, where her father was a ranger. 85

Janice Eberly, 19, will lead the 486,000- 86 member Future Farmers of America as the 87 first woman to be elected president of the 88 organization. 89

Source: Joy Stilley, "1982: Gains and Losses for American Women," Associated Press, 1983. Reprinted by permission of the publisher.

Postreading Activities
GAINS AND LOSSES FOR AMERICAN WOMEN

Part A CHECKING YOUR PREDICTIONS.   Part A of the *Prereading Activities* asked you to predict a particular achievement made by a woman that might be mentioned in the article.

Was the one you predicted mentioned?

Part B REMEMBERING FACTS.   Answer the questions on a separate piece of paper. Try to answer without looking at the story.

1. How many states had ratified the Equal Rights Amendment by the final deadline?

2. In what year was the amendment originally approved by Congress and sent to the states to vote on?

3. What new tactic did proponents decide to use in 1982?

4. What is the name of the group that led the final campaign called the ERA Countdown Campaign?

5. What did President Reagan do that was mentioned in the article?

6. What college announced that it would soon admit women students?

7. What type of material does *The Harvard Lampoon* carry?

8. Is the Actors Equity Association a social club or a union?

9. What did the Future Farmers of America do that is mentioned in the article?

Part C SCANNING FOR INFORMATION. Quickly scan the article to locate the paragraphs in which the following information is given. On a separate piece of paper, identify each paragraph by writing the number of the line in which the paragraph begins.

10. Which paragraph mentions that the ratification limit was extended?

11. Which paragraph tells how many congresswomen there were in 1980?

12. Which paragraph names an astrophysicist?

13. Which paragraph mentions an achievement that has been accomplished for a second time by a woman?

14. Which paragraph mentions an accomplishment by a woman nurse?

15. Which paragraph mentions a park in Utah?

Part D DRAWING INFERENCES. Use everyday reasoning skills to answer the following questions with either a "yes" or "no." Be prepared to explain the reasoning you used to reach each answer.

16. Do the first two sentences in the article (line 1) necessarily contradict each other?

17. Is the Constitution of the United States very easy to amend?

18. One goal of the proponents of ERA is "... to elect more women to seats in the state legislatures" (lines 17-18). Assuming they are successful, does this necessarily mean that the ERA would have a better chance of being passed if it came up for ratification again?

19. Of the 109 NOW-supported candidates at the Congressional level, 61 percent had been elected in a particular year. Does this necessarily mean that NOW support is very effective in getting people elected?

20. Does the long list of significant achievements by individual women necessarily mean that women, as a group, have achieved equity in society?

Part E DISCUSSING YOUR REACTIONS AND INSIGHTS. Consider these questions for possible discussion in the classroom.

21. Of the achievements by individual women mentioned in the article, which one do you personally consider to be the most important and why?

22. Do you think that it is right to require that an amendment be ratified by 38 of the 50 states in order for it to become part of the U.S. Consitution? Why?

Prereading Activities
THE CARE AND FEEDING OF SUPERSTITIONS

Part A MAKING PREDICTIONS.   You will be reading a true story about a number of food superstitions that are or have been widely believed. Think of a superstition or two that seem likely to be mentioned in an article that names many superstitions.

Part B UNDERSTANDING NEW WORDS.   Find the following words in the story on the lines listed below. Do not read the whole story yet, just the paragraph in which each word appears. Try to determine the meanings of the words from context. List the words on a separate piece of paper and define each.

1. obscure (line 10)
2. pertain (line 12)
3. adherents (line 13)

4. waxing (line 60)
5. waning (line 62)
6. immersed (line 69)

Part C FOCUSING YOUR READING.   Now read the entire story. While you read, think about each superstition you personally find the most unbelievable. Be prepared to discuss why you find it highly unbelievable.

While you read about the various superstitions, also think about how superstitions, in general, probably get started and why they spread.

THE CARE AND FEEDING OF SUPERSTITIONS

The last time you spilled the salt, did you take a pinch with your right hand and toss it over your left shoulder? The last time you ate an apple, did you think, "An apple a day keeps the doctor away."? 1–4

And are you careful to stir cake batters and other foods clockwise only? 5–6

These are some of the best known superstitions related to food, but they certainly are not the only ones. Being a major part of everyday life, food superstitions are numerous and varied. Some are obscure, others fairly well known; some are based on folklore; some pertain to agriculture, the growing of food. But they all have their adherents and firm believers. 7–13

Superstition has it that certain foods must be eaten on certain days to assure good luck or good fortune. 14–16

Money also has a part in a little known superstition about Easter. The belief is that you must eat duck on Easter Sunday or you will never pay your debts. 17–19

In most superstitions, the actions or beliefs either predict the coming of bad luck, or they are designed to ward off some kind of evil. 20–22

Allowing milk to boil over is supposed to produce bad luck. It's also supposed to be bad luck to give away the roots of parsley or mint, or to bake a cake on Sunday. The superstitious are warned not to throw away whole, unbroken eggs, or else a witch may come along and take them for some evil purpose. 23–29

One superstition meant to produce happiness is that of eating mince pies between Christmas and Twelfth Night. Depending on where you go, the lore calls for eating as many mince pies in as many different houses as possible, or eating a piece of mince pie every day, but no more than one piece (or it cancels out the benefit of the first piece). 30–36

For each mince pie properly applied, the belief 37

goes, you'll either have a happy day or a happy month during the coming year. 38–39

Wedding customs have their share of superstitions. Throwing rice is supposed to symbolize fertility, and the bride must be the one to cut the wedding cake or she takes the chance of being childless. 40–43

Once pregnancy is attained, food has a part in some of the superstitions involved. 44–45

The cliche, for example, of the harried husband rushing out into the night to obtain some pickles or ice cream for his pregnant wife has as much to do with superstition as accommodation. There are versions in many lands of the fairy tale that describes a pregnant woman who longed for some fruit that is out of season, and a witch was the only one who could supply her with it, on condition that the baby would be given over to be trained in witchcraft. 46–54

An unfulfilled desire for food, however, could also have its consequences. If a pregnant woman longs in vain for a particular food, it was believed that would cause the child to have a birthmark. 55–58

The moon played an important role in both determining when food should be eaten and when it should be planted. A waxing moon was considered an "up" sign and a good time to plant vegetables that grow above ground, such as corn or beans. A waning moon, however, was considered a "down sign" and perfect for planting vegetables that grow underground, such as carrots and potatoes.

The "down sign" was also considered a good time to make sauerkraut, so the cabbage would stay "down" in the bottom of the crock and remain immersed in the salty water.

Several superstitions revolve around nuts. When you find two kernels inside a nut, you're supposed to eat one of them and throw the other over your head and make a wish. After you have made the wish, you can't speak to anybody until you can answer "yes" to a question.

Agriculturally, a big crop of nuts portends a hard winter, but a poor crop means the winter will be mild. A good crop of walnuts, besides indicating a hard winter, promises a good corn harvest the following year.

Aside from keeping the doctor away, apples figure in other superstitions. In Germany, they are deemed potent against warts. In Pomerania, they are eaten on Easter morning and are considered a fever preventative. Norse gods retained their strength and youth by eating apples.

59
60
61
62
63
64
65
66
67
68
69
70
71
72
73
74
75
76
77
78
79
80
81
82
83
84
85
86
87

Source: Harvey Steiman, "The Care and Feeding of Superstitions," Knight-Ridder Newspaper Syndication, 1976. Reprinted by permission of the publisher.

Postreading Activities
THE CARE AND FEEDING OF SUPERSTITIONS

Part A CHECKING YOUR PREDICTIONS. Part A of the *Prereading Activities* asked you to predict a superstition or two that might be mentioned in the article. Many superstitions were mentioned in the article.

Were any of your predictions correct?

Part B REMEMBERING FACTS. Answer the following questions by writing "T" for "true" or "F" for "false" on a separate piece of paper. Rewrite each false statement to make it a true statement. Try to answer without looking back at the story.

T F 1. According to a superstition, cake batters and other foods should be stirred in a clockwise direction.

T F 2. According to the author, all of the superstitions he mentions are well known.

T F 3. According to a superstition, you must eat duck on Easter Sunday or you will have ill health for the rest of the year.

T F 4. According to a superstition, if a bride fails to cut the wedding cake, she runs the risk of being childless.

T F 5. According to a superstition, when you find two kernels inside a nut, you're supposed to eat both at the same time to get good luck.

T F 6. Norse gods supposedly retained their strength and youth by eating nuts.

Part C FOLLOWING STRUCTURE.   Answer the following questions on a separate piece of paper. You may go back to the story.

7. To what does "all" (line 13) refer?

8. To what does "them" (line 28) refer?

9. To what does "it" (line 35) refer?

10. To what does "it" (line 53) refer?

11. To what does "the other" (line 73) refer?

12. To what does "they" (line 84) refer?

Part D DISCUSSING YOUR REACTIONS AND INSIGHTS.   Consider these questions for possible discussion in the classroom.

13. Which of the superstitions mentioned do you personally find to be the most unbelievable? Why?

14. Speculate on some of the reasons for how superstitions get started and how they spread.

15. Think about the author's possible reason(s) for writing the article. Do you think he was trying to persuade readers to come to some conclusions regarding superstitions? Explain your reasoning.

Prereading Activities
COLLECTING GARBAGE FOR FUN AND FAME

Part A MAKING PREDICTIONS.   You will be reading a true story that has the title given above. From the title, predict whether the men you will be reading about enjoy their job.

Part B UNDERSTANDING NEW WORDS.   Find the following words in the story on the lines listed below. Do not read the whole story yet, just the paragraph in which each word appears. Try to determine the meanings of the words from the context. List the words on a separate piece of paper and define each.

1. forsaken (line 12)
2. berserk (line 20)
3. refuse (line 48)
4. flexed (line 69)

5. inhaled (line 116)
6. chronic (line 131)
7. vehicle (line 166)

Part C FOCUSING YOUR READING.   Now read the entire story. While you read, think about what you would personally like and dislike about the job described.

COLLECTING GARBAGE FOR FUN AND FAME

Berkeley, CA

Dogs barking, cans crashing, motor whining, the Mifty Lions—the crew of Truck 355 with 40,000 pounds of stinking, gooey garbage—shatter the morning quiet of the Berkeley hills with whistling, shouting and laughing.

Mifty is the old man, Lester Meredith, 42. "I've got to hang with them," he grunts. "I've got to run."

Luis Rodriquez, 32, is the captain of the team, the driver.

"A hardcore garbageman," says Mashin' Mike Ayers.

Rodriquez has even forsaken the protection of a thick leather shoulder pad and rests the hooked handle of the collection tub directly on his collarbone.

"A vet," says Mike with due reverence. Mike is the kid, at 24, new at what he calls "the sport of packing garbage."

Mashin' Mike, short and tough, takes stairs two at a time and snatches cans like a weightlifter gone berserk.

"I've got to build my rep," he says. "You've got to have the will to make it, the will to work. We go and get it. And hook it. And have fun. Like a football team. GARBAGE!"

There are 70 garbage collectors in Berkeley. But the best, exclaims Mike, are Wild Bill and Super Chicken, Billy Polk and Louis Blane. The dream team. "Awesome," says Mike.

A team too good to last. The city broke them up and made them drivers to head their own squads.

And Fred Neal. The legend. In his 60's, he uses a 95-gallon plastic tub—without wheels—on one of the hardest routes in the Berkeley hills.

"Just shows where he's coming from," says Mike. Neal trained Mike. "He gives up a lot of wisdom and knowledge."

Environmental pressures have elevated the social status of yesterday's smelly old garbage, but those who pick it up still think they don't get enough respect.

"Garbage is nasty, but someone has to do it," says Mike. "It's like picking dead people off the street. You know it will be bad so you just get down and do it. Stomp it down and hook it.

"But after you're done, you feel good, 'cause no one else can do it."

They call each other garbagemen. They like to be called refuse collectors.

"When asked, I usually say sanitation engineer. It's a little cleaner," says Lester.

Cleanliness is their obsession. They steam clean the truck at the end of the day. They steam clean the collection tubs.

"People think because we deal with garbage, we're not clean," says Mike. "But when we shower up and put on a suit, who knows who we are? 'They're just garbagemen,' they say. 'They don't have any goals.'"

Lester wears overalls to keep the refuse off his body. "You got to stay clean on this job, especially when there is a sickness going around. You got to wash your clothes real careful."

They move down Arch Street, leapfrogging each other, the man in the rear bringing the truck forward.

A good garbageman tries to do three houses without returning to the truck.

Mike grasps each can like a weightlifter. Feet spread and balanced and knees flexed, he pulls it up waist-high, then brings it up with his whole body to dump in the tub.

Crews on Berkeley trucks pick up 43,538 trash cans at 22,666 residences, according to Russell Badie, refuse division chief.

Last year, the city estimated it collected 27,888 tons of residential trash, 664 tons per garbageman or 2.75 tons per man per day.

"The average person isn't thinking about us," says Mike. "The average person is just thinking about getting this stuff out of here. Pack it. Pack it. Get rid of it. *GET IT OUT.*"

There is more trash in the summer as more people are working on their houses and yards. But cans are heavier in winter when rains soak the load.

"Rainy days are the worst," says Lester. "We've got to put the lids back on because they won't."

The garbageman knows about you. He knows when you are sick, because the level of trash drops off. He watches the way you take care of your back yard. He knows when you're down and drinking. He knows when you're doing well.

Luis hustles down a narrow concrete path beside an apartment house where three cans wait side by side. The first two are full of paper, notebooks and folders, fast-food wrappers, some orange peels, coffee grinds. "Students," he says. "They don't eat that much."

The last can has more food residue. "They have a part-time job; they're eating better," he says approvingly. "It all comes out in the garbage."

Mike is behind a large Tudor home, with a neat lawn trimmed by rose bushes. He reaches into the barrel with a gloved hand and points to an I. Magnin bag and a champagne bottle. The wet garbage is all wrapped in white plastic bags.

"Good people," he nods. "Clean people."

"Clean people" wash out their cans. They wrap their garbage. They separate the yard refuse from trash. They don't hide rocks and dirt at the bottom of the can.

"When people take care of us, we take care of them," says Luis.

Dirty people don't replace old cans, so rats and mice climb through the bottom. They don't wrap wet trash.

"Have you ever inhaled cat litter?" Mike asks.

They let maggots collect. "That's the worst," says Lester.

As the foreman/driver, Luis earns top scale of $1,843 a month. That is $84 a month more than the highest-paid collectors. All are members of Public Employees Union Local 390.

Luis' home is on this route. "He doesn't pack his garbage different than anyone else," Mike laughs.

Mike worked as a warehouseman before joining truck 355. "They break you in by sending you up in the hills, to build up your legs and wind. If you want to work, you hang with it."

Lester worked as a skilled machinist in Oakland for General Electric, where the $13-an-hour pay was good but layoffs were chronic.

"When they (Berkeley) told me I was permanent, I jumped sky high," he exclaims.

Lester Meredith weighed 240 pounds when he got the job. Now he is down to 185. "People say, 'What happened to you; you been sick?' I say no, I've been working garbage.

"People said: 'You're too old to go down there,' but I had to work, I had to take care of my family. I had to hit it.

"I love this job, I really do. On weekends, I run—you have to keep your wind. Mostly everybody down at the yard runs to keep their legs in shape.

"I tell my kids, do something different if you can. But this is all right; the City of Berkeley, I love it."

Customers pay by the can. Those in poorer areas have less money to pay for garbage pickup and they tend to have larger households and more trash.

The crew of Truck 355 prefers the hills. "The people are a little warmer to you," says Lester.

"Down in the flats, you catch all kinds of trouble. They want you to take all the extras (cans) and don't want to give you nothing. They have the money, but they are looking for something. It's not white or black, just guys looking to get away with something."

Truck 355 has a favorite customer, a woman who bakes them muffins, cupcakes and pies. "She looks after us; we look after her," says Lester. "Others set out soda pop for us on hot days, good people."

"I like working the hills. In Christmas time, we rack up," says Mike. "We get booze, money and candy."

No women work the Berkeley trucks. But that may change, supervisors say, with the purchase of a new experimental curbside vehicle designed to pick up cans in front of each house.

Garbagemen see lots of usable items in the trash,

and a lot of eatable food. They feed good meat to 169
neighborhood dogs. "We have some that follow us 170
for blocks," says Lester. 171

"This country throws away a lot of good food— 172

hams, chicken, bacon. Instead of giving it to the 173
next-door neighbor who might have a lot of kids, we 174
throw it away." 175

Source: Paul Shinoff, "Collecting Garbage—For Fun and Fame," *The San Francisco Examiner,* 1979. Reprinted by permission of the publisher.

Postreading Activities
COLLECTING GARBAGE FOR FUN AND FAME

Part A CHECKING YOUR PREDICTIONS. The answer to Part A of the *Prereading Activities* is that the men do like their job, although they do have some specific complaints.

Was your prediction on the right track?

Part B REMEMBERING FACTS. Answer the questions on a separate piece of paper. Try to answer without looking back at the story.

1. In what city do the men work?

2. What do the men call each other?

3. Name one reason why the men try to stay clean.

4. Is there more trash in the summer or winter?

5. What do the men know about students?

6. What do the men do to keep up their "wind"?

7. Why does the crew prefer the hills over the flats?

8. What do men do with the eatable food they find in the trash?

Part C FOLLOWING STRUCTURE. Answer the following questions on a separate piece of paper. You may go back to the story.

9. Who are "them" (line 7)?

10. What is the name of the "vet" (line 15)?

11. What are the names of the men on the "dream team" (lines 27 and 28)?

12. What is the full name of the "he" referred to in line 34?

13. What is "it" (line 41)?

14. What is the full name of the person speaking in lines 45 and 46?

15. Who are "they" (line 86)?

16. Who is "he" (line 90)?

17. Who are "they" (line 126)?

18. What is "it" (line 145)?

19. Who are "they" (line 152)?

20. To what does "some" (line 170) refer?

21. Who are "we" (line 174)?

Part D DRAWING INFERENCES. Use everyday reasoning skills to answer the following questions.

22. Does Mifty actually have to "run" (lines 6 and 7) because the other men are running on the job?

23. What does the term "rep" (line 21) probably refer to?

24. What kinds of "goals" (line 58) do the garbagemen probably have?

25. What would the garbage of someone who is "down and drinking" (line 90) probably be like?

26. Does "I. Magnin" (line 103) probably sell high-quality or low-quality goods?

27. What does "hang with it" (line 128) probably mean?

Part E DISCUSSING YOUR REACTIONS AND INSIGHTS. Consider these questions for possible discussion in the classroom.

28. What would you personally like and dislike about the job of garbage-man?

29. Do you think that the pay and respect that garbagemen receive is about right? Why?

30. Why do you think there are no women garbage collectors in Berkeley? Do you think it is fair not to have any? Why?

31. What would a garbageman be able to deduce about you from *your* garbage?

Prereading Activities
ABIE NATHAN'S WAR ON WAR TOYS

Part A MAKING PREDICTIONS. You will be reading a true story that has the title given above. Think about what you might do if you were leading a war on war toys, and on a separate piece of paper write the number of each of the following that you think might be mentioned in the story.

1. Talk with government officials about banning war toys.

2. Talk with store owners about not selling war toys.

3. Purchase war toys and publicly destroy them.

Part B UNDERSTANDING NEW WORDS. Below are words used in the story you are about to read. List them on a separate piece of paper. To the right of each, write its meaning, selecting from the scrambled list.

Word	*Meaning (listed in scrambled order)*
4. ceremony	A. unable to believe
5. aggressive	B. inclined to start fights or quarrels
6. profit	C. a meeting at which formal actions are conducted
7. incredulous	D. income of a business after costs are subtracted

Complete each of the following sentences by substituting one of the preceding words for the blank. The sentences are not part of the story but are given to help you understand the new words. Do NOT write on this page. Rewrite the sentences on a separate piece of paper.

8. The owners will permanently close the store if it doesn't earn a _____ this year.

9. We attended the _____ at which he was given the award.

10. When we told her of our unusual plan, she was _____ .

11. We issued a warning against continuing their _____ actions.

Part C FOCUSING YOUR READING. Now read the story. While you read, think about whether playing with war toys makes children aggressive and warlike.

ABIE NATHAN'S WAR ON WAR TOYS

Tel Aviv

"More, more!" shrieked the delighted 1
three-year-old. "Let me do it again." He took 2
the hammer and brought it down with a big 3
crash on the toy gun. Never had he enjoyed 4
himself so much with all these grownups 5
actually encouraging him to break up toys. 6

The scene was the Tel Aviv restaurant, 7
Mandy's Candy Store, in the picturesque area 8
of the old Little Tel Aviv by the old port. Abie 9
Nathan, the famous fighter for peace, who 10
mans the radio ship "The Voice of Peace" had 11
arranged a ceremony of breaking up toys 12
connected with war: toy tanks, pistols, guns, 13
etc. Children lined up to have a turn with the 14
hammer and afterwards received a certificate 15
signed by Abie that they had participated in 16
the "Smash-Up-for-Peace." 17

Abie outlined the theme behind the 18
"break-up." "I believe that we teach children 19
aggressive and warlike feelings by putting toy 20
guns into their hands. Children are not born 21
with aggressive feelings; they are more likely 22
to learn them from the TV. Suppose a Jewish 23
child plays with a Hindu or Black child and he 24
points a gun at him. If he pointed a flower or 25
candy at him, his feelings would be quite 26
different." 27

Abie has seen the Minister of Education, 28
Zevulon Hammer, about banning military 29
toys. "If Israel makes this ban, it will be the 30
first country in the world to do this," Abie 31
says. "Military toys are imported into Israel at 32
the rate of $1 million annually." 33

Does Abie have any ideas as to how this 34
million dollars could be better spent? "On 35
toys, of course," he responds. "But not war 36
toys. You make more money from non-war 37
toys. In America, the store 'Schwarz' stopped 38
selling military toys and asked some experts 39
to think up better ideas for children. The new 40
ideas were so good that the store made 300 41
percent profit that year." 42

However, the adults who gathered to 43
watch Abie's display were not so sympa- 44
thetic. "Do you really mean to break these 45
up?" asked an incredulous woman. "All that 46
money wasted." But other mothers were only 47
too anxious to join in the fun and wield the 48
hammer with the children. 49

Abie revealed that the toys going under 50
the hammer had been bought by him from 51
several Israeli shops for $500. He is trying to 52
persuade Israeli toyshops to give up selling 53
military toys entirely and offers to buy their 54
stock of these toys so that they will not lose 55
financially. Only one store, Sifri in Tel Aviv, so 56
far has agreed. The rest, according to Abie, 57
are distinctly lukewarm about the project. 58

Source: "Abie Nathan's War on War Toys," *San Francisco Jewish Bulletin*, 1977. Reprinted by permission of the publisher.

Postreading Activities
ABIE NATHAN'S WAR ON WAR TOYS

Part A CHECKING YOUR PREDICTIONS.   All three items in Part A of the *Prereading Activities* should be checked.

Which one(s) did you check?

Part B REMEMBERING FACTS.   Answer the questions on a separate piece of paper. Try to answer without looking back at the story.

1. Name one type of toy broken up in the ceremony.

2. What is the title of the government official Abie Nathan spoke with?

3. How many countries, if any, have already banned military toys?

4. How many dollars per year are spent to import military toys into Israel?

5. How did Abie obtain the toys that were broken up in the ceremony?

6. How many stores in Israel, if any, have agreed to stop selling war toys?

Part C FOLLOWING STRUCTURE.   Answer the following questions on a separate piece of paper. You may go back to the story.

7. Whose "feelings" (line 26) are being referred to?

8. To what does "it" (line 30) refer?

9. To what does "they" (line 55) refer?

10. Who are "the rest" (line 57)?

Part D DISCUSSING YOUR REACTIONS AND INSIGHTS.   Consider these questions for possible discussion in the classroom.

11. Do you think that banning war toys will help make children less aggressive? Why?

12. Do you think that Abie Nathan had children break up war toys to teach the children to be less aggressive *or* to draw publicity to his cause? Explain your reasoning.

13. If you were a parent, would there be certain types of toys that you would be reluctant to let your child play with? Explain.

Prereading Activities
GETTING IT STUCK TO YOU—AND LOVING IT

Part A MAKING PREDICTIONS.   You will be reading a true story that has the title given above. It's about acupuncture, which is a Chinese medical technique in which the body is punctured with fine, thin needles. Predict some of the types of medical problems that will be mentioned in the story.

Part B UNDERSTANDING NEW WORDS.   Below are words used in the story you are about to read. List them on a separate piece of paper. To the right of each, write its meaning, selecting from the scrambled list.

Word	Meaning (listed in scrambled order)
1. calisthenics	A. not easily persuaded or convinced; doubting
2. deteriorate	B. treatment of a disease by administration of drugs
3. chemotherapy	C. having a puncture or hole through which an organ protrudes (sticks out)
4. excruciating	D. to make or become worse
5. herniated	E. exercises meant to develop a strong, trim body
6. skeptical	F. causing very strong mental or physical pain

Complete each of the following sentences by substituting one of the preceding words for the blank. The sentences are not part of the story but are given to help you understand the new words. Do NOT write on this page. Rewrite the sentences on a separate piece of paper.

7. She faithfully performs her _____ every morning.

8. Because he did not seem trustworthy, we were very _____ about his explanation.

9. His condition began to _____ dramatically just after the unsuccessful operation.

10. When the doctor suggested _____ , she said that I would have to take the drugs four times a day.

11. When I broke my arm, the pain was _____ .

12. The doctor said I would have to undergo an operation to repair the _____ portion of my body.

Part C FOCUSING YOUR READING.   Now read the story. While you read, think about how you will personally feel about acupuncture. Think about whether you would be willing to undergo acupuncture treatment if you thought that it might help you solve a medical problem.

GETTING IT STUCK TO YOU—AND LOVING IT

Los Angeles, CA

George Harrison, the ex-Beatle, appears 1
on an eye-catching record album cover with his 2
skin pierced by slender acupuncture needles, 3
but it's not just a record-selling gimmick. 4

He actually gets acupuncture treatments— 5
a "tune-up" he calls it—whenever he visits Los 6
Angeles, he said in a recent interview. 7

Harrison, 38, is among many youth and 8
health conscious celebrities who visit Zion Yu, a 9
20th generation acupuncture practitioner in an 10
area of the country where the pursuit of happi- 11
ness produces considerable tension and torment. 12

"Why do I get acupuncture?" Harrison 13
joked at Yu's new Rejuvenation Center. "Oh 14
you know, tumors on the brain, amputated 15
legs—the run-of-the-mill diseases you pick up in 16
Hollywood." 17

Growing serious, Harrison said he learned 18
about Yu's treatments through a friend who 19
suffered a serious motorcycle injury. 20

"I thought there must be an alternative to 21
taking drugs all your life," said the famed singer- 22
guitarist with the Beatles, who has been seeing 23
Yu since 1974. 24

"He pinpoints the weak part of your system 25
and zooms in," Harrison said at a party celebrat- 26
ing the opening of Yu's new center that offers 27
acupuncture, the concentrated exercise Tai 28
Chi calisthenics, massage and skin treatments. 29

Yu has practiced acupuncture in Los 30
Angeles for 10 years since coming from Taiwan 31
and his patients include actors William Holden, 32
James Coburn, James Garner and William 33
Shatner, entertainer Merv Griffin, actresses 34

Jane Fonda and Natalie Wood, and singer 35
Peggy Lee. 36

Other celebrities have asked Yu not to dis- 37
close their names, he said. 38

Yu, 35, uses the 5,000-year-old Chinese 39
medical treatment for all kinds of ailments— 40
arthritis, depression, loss of hair. He even offers 41
acupuncture "face lifts" that he claims tighten 42
facial tissue. 43

"Everything in the body is based on the 44
nerves," Yu said. "When they deteriorate, the 45
body energy flow doesn't supply enough mes- 46
sages to the memory bank and everything slows 47
down. We stimulate the nervous system prop- 48
erly and the weak part gets stronger. People 49
look better, their memory is better, and they are 50
happier and willing to do more things." 51

Yu advises his patients to accept acupunc- 52
ture as something that will help them. Their 53
mental attitude toward the treatment is impor- 54
tant, he said. 55

"Many people think this is a gimmick or 56
something. Wrong. People who experience this 57
know. They feel the changes released through- 58
out their entire system." 59

His patients claim he has cured uncomfort- 60
able chemotherapy symptoms, increased their 61
hair growth, and heightened their body sensi- 62
tivity. 63

"The whole thing is different from Ameri- 64
can medicine," said Gary Steffen, 57, a ruddy- 65
faced businessman who suffered from back 66
trouble, skin cancer on his hand and ulcers. 67

"Zion doesn't claim to cure cancer, but 68
after the treatment the redness and itching went 69
away, and those were the cancer symptoms," 70
Steffen said, rubbing his right hand. 71

Larry Sears, 38, said he had suffered ex- 72
cruciating pain from a herniated disc and was 73
"hallucinating" on morphine. Doctors had recom- 74
mended surgery when Sears heard of Yu's clinic 75
2and decided to try it. 76

"I was in tears when I came to Zion," he 77
said. "But 45 minutes after my first treatment, 78
my pain was gone." 79

The pain returned, but so did Sears, and 80
within 60 days he was virtually cured, he said. 81

Writer Maurice Zolotow, 67, started get- 82
ting acupuncture for a painful wrenched back 83
and was skeptical at first. 84

"I was very much afraid of it. I would 85
scream as every needle went in. But most of it 86
was in my mind. Every pain went away." 87

Now he visits the clinic every two weeks for 88
"balancing" treatment, in which Yu inserts nee- 89
dles in various parts of the body, "to keep me 90
feeling good." 91

"Insertion of the needles takes just a few 92
minutes," Zolotow said. "Then you lie in semi- 93
darkness for 20 minutes. Acupuncture prevents 94
blockage and permits the free flow of energy." 95

Thelma Walker, 59, executive secretary to 96
Mo Ostin, chairman of Warner Brothers Records 97
Inc., suffered agonizing chemotherapy effects 98
during a bout with cancer three years ago. 99

"Nobody knows how bad you feel when 100
you're on chemotherapy," she said. Then she 101
experienced Yu's needles. "It was so nice not to 102
have to take a drug and worry about the side 103
effects," she said. 104

Spinal arthritis also plagued her and putting 105
on her clothes was a painful, time-consuming 106
chore. 107

"For nine months I could not raise my 108
hands. But the first treatment with Zion took the 109
pain away," she said. "After he puts the pins in, 110
you float. I've never been that high." 111

Postreading Activities
GETTING IT STUCK TO YOU—AND LOVING IT

Part A CHECKING YOUR PREDICTIONS.   Part A of the *Prereading Activities* asked you to predict some of the types of medical problems that will be mentioned in the story. Many were mentioned.

Were any of your predictions correct?

Part B REMEMBERING FACTS.   Answer the questions on a separate piece of paper. Try to answer without looking back at the story.

1. What is the name of the musical group to which George Harrison used to belong?

2. Where does Zion Yu practice acupuncture?

3. What is the name of one celebrity, other than George Harrison, who is named in the story?

4. According to Yu, what does acupuncture do the the the nerves?

5. Does Yu claim to cure cancer?

6. How often does the man who has a painful wrenched back visit Yu?

7. How long does it take to insert the needles?

8. What did acupuncture do for the woman who was suffering chemotherapy effects?

Part C FOLLOWING STRUCTURE.   Answer the following questions on a separate piece of paper. You may go back to the story.

9. To what does "it" (line 4) refer?

10. What is the full name of the "he" referred to in line 5?

11. What is the full name of the "he" referred to in line 25?

12. To what does "this" (line 57) refer?

13. What is the full name of the person whose "pain" is referred to in line 79?

14. What is the full name of the "he" who is referred to in line 88?

15. What is the full name of the "she" who is referred to in line 110?

Part D SCANNING FOR INFORMATION. Quickly scan the story to locate the paragraphs in which the following information is given. Identify each paragraph by writing the number of the line in which the paragraph begins on a separate piece of paper.

16. Which paragraph tells that Harrison was interviewed at a party?

17. Which paragraph tells how long acupuncture has been in use?

18. Which paragraph names some cancer symptoms?

19. Which paragraph tells the name of Thelma Walker's employer?

20. Which paragraph tells how long Thelma Walker could not raise her hands?

Part E DISCUSSING YOUR REACTIONS AND INSIGHTS. Consider these questions for possible discussion in the classroom.

21. How do you personally feel about receiving acupuncture treatments? Would you be willing to undergo acupunture treatment if you thought it might help you solve a medical problem?

22. Do you think that Harrison's joke about why he gets acupuncture (see lines 14-17) is funny? Why?

Prereading Activities
DICK GREGORY STARVES TO AID HUNGER FIGHT

Part A MAKING PREDICTIONS.   You will be reading a story that has the title given above. Try to predict how it is possible for someone to help medical researchers by starving himself.

Part B UNDERSTANDING NEW WORDS.   Below are scrambled definitions of words used in the story you are about to read. Unscramble the definitions by rearranging the phrases. Phrases are separated by double slashes (//). Then write a sentence using each word.

1.   **monitor** (verb) in order to // check systematically // certain types of information // collect

2.   **resiliency** (noun) from illness, change, etc. // to recover // the ability

3.   **haute cuisine** (noun, French) prepared // fine food / highly skilled // by // chefs

4.   **metabolize** (verb) food // so it can be used // to break down

5.   **internist** (noun) who studies and // a physician // treats non-surgical internal diseases

Part C FOCUSING YOUR READING.   Now read the story. While you read, think about whether you would volunteer to do what Dick Gregory is doing. Why?

DICK GREGORY STARVES TO AID HUNGER FIGHT

New Orleans

An unusual experiment in one of the best cities 1
for fine dining may yield scientific data on the process 2
of human starvation. 3

Black activist Dick Gregory is in the eighth 4
week of a fast monitored by doctors at Dillard Uni- 5
versity's Flint Goodridge Hospital. Gregory, who 6
proposed the experiment, said he hopes the data 7
collected will help the fight against world hunger. 8

"You can pay some people to climb the Empire 9
State Building or the Sears Tower, but you can't pay 10
anyone to go 56 or 70 days without eating," Gregory 11
said of his reason for volunteering for the experiment. 12

Dr. Joseph Allain, director of the team monitor- 13
ing Gregory, said the research has implications for 14
world diet and eating habits. Rising food prices may 15
make people look at the difference between food 16
intake and nutrition, Allain said. 17

Orthomolecular nutrition, the study of mole- 18
cules and compounds needed to fulfill the metabolic 19
needs of the body, is receiving more scholarly atten- 20
tion. The study may lead people to rethink the 21
amount of protein, especially meat, they need to eat. 22
Allain said. 23

"We don't have to panic that after six hours of 24
not eating we have to throw something in our stom- 25
achs," Allain said. 26

Allain said that Gregory demonstrated his resili- 27
ency recently while attending the funeral of former 28
NAACP leader Roy Wilkins in New York. The 29
medical monitoring team accompanied him on the 30
trip. Airplane takeoffs and landings adversely affected 31
Gregory's vital signs, but the doctors said his recovery 32
was quick. 33

Gregory, a veteran of hunger strikes for political 34
purposes, said he is sorry that hunger strikers in 35
Ireland do not know more about nutrition. 36

"I think it would serve their cause better if they 37
were doing it right," Gregory said. "The strikers' 38
biggest problem is taking salt tablets, which interfere 39
with liver and kidney functions," he said. 40

Gregory said that although he saw hunger 41
strikes as a possible political weapon for the 80's, the 42
problem of world hunger drove him to undertake the 43
experiment. 44

"Twenty-eight people starve to death every 45
minute on this planet, and most of them are women 46
and children," Gregory said. 47

The walls of Gregory's private hospital room are 48
covered with pictures of hamburgers, haute cuisine 49
and nature scenes. A completed jigsaw puzzle depict- 50
ing a glass of milk and chocolate cookies hangs at the 51
foot of his bed. 52

Researchers are studying what adaptations the 53
body makes to prolonged starvation. 54

In the early phases of starvation the body gets 55
energy from stored fat, but after the tissue is con- 56
sumed it metabolizes protein to survive. Allain said 57
Gregory's metabolism is diminishing because "it 58
knows it's getting closer and closer to the point where 59
it can't give up any more protein." 60

The researchers also are testing the role of 61
endorphins in the starvation process. Endorphins are 62
newly discovered chemicals produced in the brain 63
that are believed to increase the body's tolerance to 64
pain and trauma. 65

Doctors have expressed concern that Gregory 66
could seem to be doing well but actually could be 67
passing a "point of no return" where permanent 68
damage occurs. After each morning physical, the 69
doctors decide whether to let Gregory continue his 70
fast. 71

Skin tests on a regular basis "challenge" Gregory's 72

system, so doctors can determine if vital antigens are being broken down by the starving body. 73 74

At day 56, Gregory was experiencing no vitamin deficiencies despite loss of 42 pounds and a 33 percent drop in body fat. Doctors are quick to point out that Gregory came to them an "ideal specimen" who is a "professional at fasting." 75 76 77 78 79

Gregory has suffered none of the loss of body functions that plagued Irish hunger strikers in the days before their deaths. Bobby Sands, for example, died in the 66th day of his fast. 80 81 82 83

To demonstrate his health, Gregory plans to walk from New Orleans to Baton Rouge—about 90 miles—on the 70th day of his fast. Assuming approval by the medical team, he will break his fast and begin walking. His only nutrition will be a protein pack Gregory will prepare for himself. 84 85 86 87 88 89

The team monitoring Gregory's progress includes Allain, an internist, Dr. James Carter, chief of the chair of nutrition at Tulane Medical School, Dr. Len Simon, a psychiatrist, and Dr. Pat Galloway, a psychologist. 90 91 92 93 94

Source: "Dick Gregory Starves to Aid Hunger Fight," *The Dallas Morning News*, 1981. Reprinted by permission of the publisher.

Postreading Activities
DICK GREGORY STARVES TO AID HUNGER FIGHT

Part A CHECKING YOUR PREDICTIONS. The answer to Part A of the *Prereading Activities* is that by starving himself while being observed by physicians, Dick Gregory can contribute to knowledge about the process of starvation. By knowing more about the process of starvation, doctors will be better able to help those who are involuntarily at various stages of starvation.

Was your prediction correct?

Part B REMEMBERING FACTS. Answer the questions on a separate piece of paper. Try to answer without looking back at the story.

1. In what city is the experiment being conducted?

2. Who proposed the experiment?

3. Why has Gregory gone on hunger strikes in the past?

4. What does Gregory say the Irish hunger strikers are doing wrong?

5. What does Gregory have hanging on the walls of his hospital room?

6. From what does the body get its energy in the early stages of starvation?

7. How often is Gregory given a physical exam?

8. What does Gregory plan to do on the 70th day of his fast?

Part C FOLLOWING STRUCTURE. Answer the following questions on a separate piece of paper. You may go back to the story.

9. To whom does "his" (line 27) refer?

10. Who is "he" (line 35)?

11. To what does "it" (line 38) refer?

12. To what does "it" (line 58) refer?

13. What is Bobby Sands' nationality? (line 82)

14. What is the name of the "psychiatrist" (line 93)?

Part D IDENTIFYING MAIN IDEAS. Answer each question by selecting the best choice. You may refer to the story.

15. Which of the following best expresses the main idea of the paragraph that begins on line 13?

    A. Food prices are rising around the world.
    B. Doctors such as Dr. Allain have a keen interest in the process of starvation because of their scientific curiosity.
    C. The study has implications for world diet and eating habits.

16. Which sentence in the paragraph that begins on line 27 best expresses the main idea of the paragraph?

    A. The first sentence in the paragraph.
    B. The second sentence in the paragraph.
    C. The third sentence in the paragraph.

17. Which sentence in the paragraph that begins on line 66 best expresses the main idea of the paragraph?

    A. The first sentence in the paragraph.
    B. The second sentence in the paragraph.

18. Which sentence in the paragraph that begins on line 84 best expresses the main idea of the paragraph?

    A. The first sentence in the paragraph.

    B. The second sentence in the paragraph.

    C. The third sentence in the paragraph.

Part E DISCUSSING YOUR REACTIONS AND INSIGHTS.   Consider these questions for possible discussion in the classroom.

19. Would you be willing to volunteer to do what Dick Gregory is doing? Why?

20. Do you think it will serve any useful function for Gregory to walk from New Orleans to Baton Rouge on the 70th day of his fast? Why?

21. Do you think that what doctors learn about the process of starvation by studying Gregory will apply to all other humans? Why?

Prereading Activities
A FOOD SAMPLER OF STRANGE THINGS TO EAT

Part A MAKING PREDICTIONS. You will be reading a true story that has the title given above. Think about things you think might be "strange" to eat and predict the names of one or two odd foods that probably will be mentioned in the story.

Part B UNDERSTANDING NEW WORDS. Below are scrambled definitions of words used in the story you are about to read. Unscramble the definitions by rearranging the phrases. Phrases are separated by double slashes (//). Then write a sentence using each word.

1. **cornucopia** (noun) of food // an abundance // often displayed in a goat's horn

2. **culinary** (adjective) or to cookery // relating // to a kitchen

3. **exotic** (adjective) of the // the charm // unfamiliar // having

4. **litany** (noun) that is often // a statement // long and repetitive

5. **intact** (adjective) cut up // not impaired // in any way // or

6. **pungent** (adjective) or smelling // tasting // strong and sharp

7. **palate** (noun) of // sense // taste // the

Part C FOCUSING YOUR READING. Now read the story. While you read, select the one "strange" food mentioned that you've never eaten before but would most like to sample. Think about your reason for your selection.

A FOOD SAMPLER OF STRANGE THINGS TO EAT

There are strange things to eat in foreign lands. Things which seldom grace the table at home. It is true that food in foreign countries is most often a high point of the trip. The pasta of Italy, the cheeses of France, the whipped-cream-smothered desserts of Germany and the cornucopia of tropical fruit in the Philippines are some of the things which come to mind.

But there are other sorts of food that make most travelers shrink from the table. Such things as snake soup, duck tongues, some interior part of the pig or the black chile sauces of Mexico might be numbered by some as the absolute pits, from a culinary standpoint.

There are also those occasions when the food looks good and tastes good—until some helpful person tells what you're really eating and ruins an otherwise nice meal. And it doesn't have to be really exotic food. According to one woman traveler I know, being told she had just dined on breast of dove turned her off from any kind of fowl for several months.

Sauces and spices can also ruin a meal. Just the idea of octopus served in its own ink can send people running for the next plane home. The hidden heat in the innocent bits of red pepper which decorate a Thai dish of shrimp can make you wonder whether you'll last through the tour, or even to dessert.

Misadventures with food can often seem funny—years later. But at the time the pain of discovery can be physical and emotional. I once saw a man in a Hong Kong restaurant throw down his chopsticks in disgust when told he was eating pigeon. "My God," he choked, "we keep them as pets at home."

I have some idea of how he felt. Some Chinese friends in Hong Kong invited me to dine with them. They said they had ordered a meal with several special dishes. The first special dish consisted of what I assumed to be chicken legs in a lovely sweet-and-sour sauce.

"What is it?" I said, already sure of the answer. "Guess," answered the hostess. "Chicken legs?" "No, not at all," was the reply. That was followed by a litany of chicken parts. All received a negative response. "Tell me, please." "Those are duck tongues," she said.

The look on my face must have been an absolute study. "Don't you like it?" What can you do? Yes, it was good—until I found out what it was. How do you smile and gag at the same time? And, besides all that turmoil, my mind was filled with the question of how many ducks had died for the six of us to enjoy this "special" dish.

It is at times like that when I admire travelers who say very simply and clearly: "Ducks' tongues? No, I don't like it. The idea of it makes me sick. Do you think I can order a chopped steak?" Instead, most swallow, reach for more of the special dish and try to forget the last time they saw a quacking duck waddle across the farmyard.

The bat of Guam, a local delicacy, belongs with duck tongues. The difference between the two is that the duck tongues are hard to spot but the bat, prepared as soup, is still intact when served up. Only extremely bad vision would permit anyone to pick up the soup spoon.

But there are many strange things served up in foreign lands that are a delight—although some of it might fall into the category of "pets." Young goat, or kid, is a popular dish in the north of Italy. Stewed slowly in a tomato sauce and served over a mound of boiled corn meal, it is a dish designed for the hearty appetites of the Alpine folk who invented it.

France is a country where snails are everyday fare. The snails, I am convinced, are used only as

an excuse to consume the heavenly sauce of melted 75
butter and garlic in which they are served. (The 76
French also use the goat—not for its meat, but the 77
milk that produces a range of pungent cheeses.) 78

A few years ago, when beef prices were high, 79
horse meat enjoyed a brief popularity in the United 80
States. In France, there are shops—marked by a gold 81
horse head carving over the front door—which deal 82
exclusively in horse meat. And in the fall and winter, 83
it can be found on restaurant menus. Horse meat, it is 84
believed, can keep you warm and cold free in the 85
harsher months. 86

The Chinese do not subscribe to that belief. In 87
China, the warming winter dish is snake soup. There 88
is even a poem about it with the opening lines 89
referring to winter time being the season for the five 90
types of snake used in making the soup. 91

Another specialty of the Chinese is the pigeon at 92
that already mentioned Hong Kong restaurant. The 93
menu calls it squab to give a certain dignity to the 100 94
different ways in which it is prepared. No, they do not 95
serve pigeon tongues. 96

The hot spices used in cooking in parts of the 97
world can often be a greater danger than the distress 98
caused by finding out you've eaten part of a strange 99
animal. In Thailand, where peppers used in seasoning 100
often mask the food completely (for those unused to 101
it), the spicy heat can strip your mouth. Icy cold 102
beverages are the best to ease the pain. Stay away 103
from hot tea, it only makes it worse. 104

Mexico offers a wide selection of heat for the 105
palate. But many of the chile-based sauces are milder 106
than they appear. The black *mole,* for example, is not 107
as deadly as it appears. The flavors of different chiles 108
work well with the breast of wild turkey that is a 109
regular on restaurant menus. 110

The hottest meal I have ever had was in Cebu, in 111
the Philippines. It was fish steamed and served with 112
tiny, orange chile peppers. One bite of that innocent 113
looking pepper was the end of the meal for me. It 114
seared the mouth, the throat—I felt it all the way 115
down to my feet. Bottles of cold beer, followed by 116
glass after glass of ice water did little to kill the fire. It 117
was three days before I could again taste anything. 118

Friends from the Philippines tell me that those 119
tiny bombshell peppers are actually mild in compari- 120
son with some served in the southern islands of the 121
western Pacific. "Besides," they add, "it's all in your 122
mind. If you know before you eat that the peppers are 123
hot, it's easy to eat them." 124

As a result of many culinary surprises, I now 125
find it a good idea to do a little research about a 126
country's food before traveling there for the first time. 127
One of the best sources for food research—written 128
for the American palate—is the Time-Life "Foods of 129
the World" series. If you haven't read anything before 130
you go, try to buy a cookbook in English once you 131
arrive. Besides telling about foods you may not want 132
to try, locally-produced cooking and food books can 133
serve as an excellent menu guide. 134

Source: Richard Paoli, "A Food Sampler," *San Francisco Examiner,* 1982. Reprinted by permission of the publisher.

Postreading Activities
A FOOD SAMPLER OF STRANGE THINGS TO EAT

Part A CHECKING YOUR PREDICTIONS. Part A of the *Prereading Activities* asked you to predict the names of some "strange" foods that might be mentioned in the story. Were you successful in predicting any of the many types of unusual foods mentioned?

Part B REMEMBERING FACTS.   Answer the following questions by selecting the best choice for each. Try to answer without looking back at the story.

1.   The author mentions the cheeses of what country?

   A.   Italy   B.   Germany   C.   France

2.   The author mentions the smothered desserts of what country?

   A.   Italy   B.   Germany   C.   France

3.   A woman traveler was "turned off from any kind of fowl" after she discovered she had eaten which of the following?

   A.   chicken necks   B.   breast of dove   C.   octopus

4.   Why was the man in the Hong Kong restaurant angry about the pigeon dish he was served?

   A.   Where he came from, pigeons are kept as pets.

   B.   The dish was too spicy and burned his throat.

   C.   The pigeon was mixed with a sauce he didn't like.

5.   According to the author, snails are eaten everyday in what country?

   A.   France   B.   Italy   C.   China

6.   According to the author, which of the following enjoyed a brief popularity in the United States?

   A.   breast of dove   B.   horse meat   C.   snake soup

7.   What does the author suggest that you do if you accidentally eat food with peppers that you find to be too hot?

   A.   Drink some hot tea.

   B.   Drink some room-temperature water.

   C.   Drink icy cold beverages.

8.   Where did the author find the hottest meal he ever had?

   A.   France

   B.   The Philippines

   C.   Mexico

9.   What does the author suggest you do to avoid food surprises when going to a country for the first time?

   A.   Eat only in hotel restaurants once you arrive.

B. Do some research on the country's food before you travel there.

C. Rent a small apartment so that you can cook your own food.

Part C FOLLOWING STRUCTURE.   Answer the following questions on a separate piece of paper. You may go back to the story.

10. Did the hostess or the writer say "No, not at all" (lines 41 and 42)?

11. Did the hostess or the writer say "Tell me, please" (line 44)?

12. To what does "it" (line 55) refer?

13. To what does "it" (line 89) refer?

14. To what does "it" (line 114) refer?

Part D IDENTIFYING MAIN IDEAS.   Answer the following questions on a separate piece of paper. You may refer to the story.

15. In the paragraph that begins on line 15, which sentence (1st, 2nd, or 3rd) best expresses the main idea of the paragraph?

16. In the paragraph that begins on line 22, which sentence (1st, 2nd, or 3rd) best expresses the main idea of the paragraph?

17. In the paragraph that begins on line 87, which sentence (1st, 2nd, or 3rd) best expresses the main idea of the paragraph?

Part E DISCUSSING YOUR REACTIONS AND INSIGHTS.   Consider these questions for possible discussion in the classroom.

18. Name the one "strange" food that you've never eaten before but would like most to sample. Give a reason for your choice.

19. Why is it that a food that seems "strange" to one group of people doesn't seem strange to another group?

20. Why is it that most people continue eating a dish even though they've found out that it contains a food that they'd rather not eat? (See paragraph that begins on line 53.)

21. What one type of food are you most sure that you'll never eat because you find the idea of it repulsive? Why do you feel this way about the type of food you named?

22. What type of food did you hate to try but were surprised to find that you enjoyed?

Prereading Activities
A NOAH'S ARK SURVIVAL PLAN FOR IMPERILED SPECIES

Part A MAKING PREDICTIONS.   You will be reading a true story that has the title given above. The story is about a plan to save species of animals that are threatened with extinction. From the title, infer whether there are many or few imperiled species.

Part B UNDERSTANDING NEW WORDS.   Below are words used in the story you are about to read. List them on a separate piece of paper. To the right of each, write its meaning, selecting from the scrambled list.

Word	*Meaning (listed in scrambled order)*
1. curator	A. the act of working together, especially on a difficult project
2. criteria	
3. collaboration	B. the region where a plant or animal naturally lives
4. obstacle	C. a person in charge of a museum, zoo, etc.
5. habitat	
6. innovative	D. being a new method, often creative
7. propagate	E. to reproduce itself, usually said of a plant or animal
8. inbred	F. coming from closely related parents
	G. the standards by which something is to be judged
	H. anything that gets in the way

Complete each of the following sentences by substituting one of the preceding words for the blank. The sentences are not part of the story but are given to help you understand the new words. (Do NOT write on this page. Rewrite the sentences on a separate piece of paper.)

9.   Her strong objections were a major _____ to carrying out our plan.

10.   We went to the national forest to observe the birds in their _____ .

11.   He received a pay raise for his _____ solution to the problem.

12.   We had a party to celebrate the fact that she had just been named the new _____ of the museum.

13.   This type of dog is so _____ that many of the offspring are highly nervous and unreliable.

14. We asked her if we could have seeds from the plant so that we could _____ them ourselves.

15. We suggested that the screenwriter work in _____ with the musician on the new play.

16. In the job announcement, the company listed the _____ for being selected for promotion.

Part C FOCUSING YOUR READING.   Now read the story. While you read, think about whether you personally think enough is being done to save imperiled species.

A NOAH'S ARK SURVIVAL PLAN FOR IMPERILED SPECIES

Dallas, TX

The list reads like a Who's Who for Noah's ark.

The cast includes a host of exotic individuals: Preezewlski's horse, Humboldt's penguin, Grevy's zebra, lion-tailed Macaque monkey, Madagascan brown boa and the gray, nondescript Coahuilan box turtle.

The rare species are among a select group chosen for preservation. But instead of boarding a ship two-by-two, their last refuge is in zoos.

They are part of a Species Survival Plan, a "program of last resort" akin to zoologists playing God, said John Wortman, curator of mammals at the Dallas Zoo.

Wortman is one of hundreds of zoologists in the American Association of Zoological Parks and Aquariums, which set up the survival program in the last-ditch effort to save certain species from extinction.

"One of the problems that occurs is, which species do you pick to save?" said Elvie Turner, Jr., director of the Fort Worth Zoo and a representative to the survival plan project, which was set up about two years ago.

"One of the criteria is that they have to be endangered in the wild, but we wouldn't take on a species that has no chance of successfully reproducing in captivity."

The project, the only one of its kind, involves a breeding program for selected endangered species in North American zoos. So far, 30 species are included in the program; more are to be added.

The survival plan's long-term goal is not just to keep the animals alive in zoos, but to repopulate Earth with them someday—even if on protected wildlife refuges.

"So many species are being lost that the problem of choosing those which could be sustained in the survival plan is difficult," said William Conway, project chairman and director of the Bronx Zoo.

The zoologists are working against time— Conway estimates that as many as 1 million plant and animal species will become extinct in the next 15 years—and their goal is enormously complex and expensive.

About 250 animals of each species are necessary to maintain a healthy breeding pool of animals, zoologists say.

"It is necessary to keep large groups of 52
animals so that species are genetically sound," 53
Conway said. "The whole key is collaboration 54
and research. While no zoo would want 250 55
lowland gorillas or Siberian tigers, it may be 56
possible for all zoos in America and other 57
countries to keep that many and move them 58
back and forth for breeding purposes." 59

Shipping the animals between zoos is a 60
major obstacle. Transporting one rhino can 61
cost as much as $4,000. 62

But time is running out for many species. 63
Not because man is openly killing them, but 64
because man is destroying their habitat. 65

Although zoos are the only salvation for 66
many endangered animals, "at the very most" 67
only a few thousand species can be saved, 68
Conway said. 69

Meanwhile, the role of zoos is no longer 70
to act simply as tourist attractions. Zoos are 71
maintaining fewer species and building up a 72
larger selection of individual species, in cooper- 73
ation with species preservation objectives. 74

Like others, the Dallas Zoo has reduced 75
its variety of species and is specializing in 76
breeding programs for several endangered 77
species, including the African black rhino. 78

"We aren't capable of holding all the 79
species, so we are specializing and making a 80

commitment to a few. It also lets us partici- 81
pate in the research," Wortman said. 82

Some specialization is a learn-as-you-go 83
process. 84

Dallas zoologists, for example, learned 85
the hard way that a certain antelope species 86
will not reproduce as quickly if the animals 87
are herded together. 88

"We found that there is a hierarchy of 89
females, and that to get them to reproduce, 90
we have to introduce them separately to the 91
males," Wortman said. "Behavior sometimes 92
alters physiology." 93

Zoologists are looking at innovative ways 94
to increase the chances for building a larger 95
gene pool of animals. One project involves a 96
Texas rancher who maintains breeding herds 97
of Grevy's zebra and black rhino for partici- 98
pating zoos. 99

"The ranch program has worked out 100
remarkably well," said Turner, who coordi- 101
nates the pilot project. "We are sending stock 102
to propagate a group with varied backgrounds. 103
We can't do that in zoos, but with that much 104
property, ranchers can. 105

"In the past, zoo animals were inbred 106
and lost a lot of their genetic characteristics, 107
and the animals all turned out alike," Turner 108
said. "In the wild, the characteristics are all 109
mixed up, and that's what we want." 110

Source: Esther M. Bauer, "A Noah's Ark Survival Plan for Imperiled Species," *The Dallas Morning News*, 1983. Reprinted by permission of the publisher.

Postreading Activities
A NOAH'S ARK SURVIVAL PLAN FOR IMPERILED SPECIES

Part A CHECKING YOUR PREDICTIONS. Part A of the *Prereading Activities* asked you to infer from the title whether there are many or few imperiled species. The answer, in the article, is that there are many.

Was your inference correct?

Part B REMEMBERING FACTS. Answer the questions on a separate piece of paper. Try to answer without looking back at the story.

1. About how long ago was the survival plan project established?

2. Why does the plan reject some imperiled species?

3. About how many species have been included in the plan so far?

4. About how many animals of each species are needed to maintain a healthy breeding pool?

5. How much can it cost to transport one rhino from zoo to zoo?

6. What innovative approach is described in the article?

7. What undesirable thing tended to happen in the past when zoos bred animals?

Part C FOLLOWING STRUCTURE. Answer the following questions on a separate piece of paper. You may go back to the story.

8. To what does "they" (line 12) refer?

9. What is the full name of the person who is being quoted in the paragraph that begins on line 21?

10. What is the full name of the person who is being quoted in the paragraph that begins on line 52?

11. To whom does "them" (line 91) refer?

12. What is the full name of the person who is being quoted in the last paragraph?

Part D SCANNING FOR INFORMATION. Quickly scan the story to locate the paragraphs in which the following information is given. Identify each paragraph by writing the number of the line in which the paragraph begins on a separate piece of paper.

13. Which paragraph names the continent on which the survival plan is currently being carried out?

14. Which paragraph names the number of plant and animal species that will become extinct in the next 15 years?

15. Which paragraph tells what man is doing that is causing some animals to become extinct?

16. Which paragraph tells that zoos are maintaining few species?

Part E DISCUSSING YOUR REACTIONS AND INSIGHTS. Consider these questions for possible discussion in the classroom.

17. Do you personally think that enough is being done to save imperiled species? Why?

18. If you were asked to make a personal contribution of several dollars to the survival plan, would you probably contribute? Why?

19. Why would no one zoo want 250 lowland gorillas or 250 Siberian tigers?

20. Which is more important—the survival of threatened species or the development of land for use by humans? Is there a middle road? Explain your answer.

Prereading Activities
CHARLIE PARKHURST: THE STAGECOACH DRIVER WITH A SECRET

Part A MAKING PREDICTIONS.   You will be reading a story that has the title given above. Here are some hints to Charlie's secret:

    A.   Charlie was never married.

    B.   Charlie's friends did not know any of Charlie's relatives.

    C.   There is something misleading about Charlie's name.

    D.   Charlie's secret was not discovered until Charlie was being dressed for burial.

    1.   Guess what Charlie's secret is. After you've read the story, check to see if your guess is correct.

Part B UNDERSTANDING NEW WORDS.   Below are words used in the story you are about to read. List them on a separate piece of paper. To the right of each, write its meaning, selecting from the scrambled list.

Word	Meaning (listed in scrambled order)
2. comply	A. typically untalkative or uncommunicative
3. veer	B. to act in accordance with a command, request, rule, etc.
4. taciturn	C. the cause of destruction or ruin
5. fledgling	D. to turn aside from a course or direction
6. dub	E. young and inexperienced
7. insulate	F. to nickname
8. ironic	G. clearly different from what might be expected; what is strange in contrast with what might be expected
9. bane	H. to detach or isolate
10. wiry	I. lean and slender but tough

Complete each of the following sentences by substituting one of the preceding words for the blank. The sentences are not part of the story but are given to help you understand the new words. (Do NOT write on this page. Rewrite the sentences on a separate piece of paper.)

    11.   We noticed the large rock in the road just in time to _____ around it.

12. We told our employer that it would be difficult to _____ with the new rules without additional employees to help us.

13. The new teacher was clearly a _____ .

14. Because he was only four feet tall, we were tempted to _____ him "Shorty."

15. She came across as the strong, silent type because she was so _____ even at parties.

16. We thought it _____ that he worked so hard in school yet got poor grades.

17. The _____ little animal was able to squeeze through the tiny hole in the fence.

18. We were able to _____ ourselves from the cold air by piling old rags on ourselves.

19. We agreed that his drinking problem would become the _____ of his existence.

Part C FOCUSING YOUR READING. Now read the story. While you read, think about what you personally would and would not like about Charlie's job if you were Charlie.

CHARLIE PARKHURST:
The Stagecoach Driver with a Secret

California

"Throw down the box."　1

This was the standard command of the high-　2
wayman in Gold Rush days.　3

The first time driver Charlie Parkhurst heard　4
those words at a turn in the road, he grudgingly　5
complied.　6

The next time—well, the next time when a gang　7
of highway robbers jumped from behind some　8
bushes, Parkhurst reacted so fast there wasn't *time* for　9
a command. Parkhurst fired his shotgun first, hitting　10
the leader, then veered his team of six horses toward　11
the others, making a deep impression that crime does　12
not pay—not with this driver.　13

Passengers aboard the Concord coach swiftly　14
spread the word after they reached town. It may have　15
been that news or just plain luck, but never again did　16
a bandit try to get the drop on the taciturn, tobacco-　17
chewing driver.　18

His career spanned thirty years, two-thirds of it　19
in California during the frenzied time when gold fever　20
demanded rapid transit. And the 5-foot, 7-inch tall　21
Parkhurst delivered.　22

Station agents would say, "That's Old Charlie　23
coming in. He's right on time."　24

Being "right on time" became Parkhurst's trade-　25
mark after he joined Jim Burch's fledgling California　26
Stage Lines. Parkhurst's knack for handling horses　27
led stable hands to say, "He uses some kind of　28
hoodoo."　29

The slender driver, dubbed "Old Charlie"　30
because he was nearly 40 when he came West in　31
1851, also knew how to handle the Concord coach, a　32
graceful, 2,500-pound vehicle.　33

Parkhurst's skills were needed. Narrow, wind-　34
ing Mother Lode roads, pocked with mire or hub-deep　35

in dust, proved a bigger hazard than highwaymen.　36
Layers of poles and brush were corduroyed on the　37
mush spots of roads between the towns and cities　38
where he delivered passengers, mail and payrolls.　39

He could turn a six-horse hitch and coach in a　40
street at full gallop with every line loose. He became　41
something of a legend in the days when "the average　42
stage driver was above all, lord in his way, the captain　43
of his craft, the fear of timid passengers, the admira-　44
tion of the stable boys, and the trusted agent of his em-　45
ployer," said historian Hubert H. Bancroft.　46

Once, in the middle of a bridge spanning the　47
rushing Tuolumne River, Parkhurst and his pas-　48
sengers felt the old structure wobbling. Instantly, the　49
driver's whip sounded the alarm, punctuated by　50
language salty enough to sting. The coach reached the　51
bank just as the bridge collapsed behind it.　52

Some stagecoach drivers earned their reputa-　53
tions for their swagger or the risks they ran, often　54
insulated from fear by whiskey.　55

When Old Charlie was captain of the Concord,　56
the passengers relaxed.　57

Oh, he drank some after a run, but he never　58
tipped a bottle before or during one, which helps　59
explain why no one ever got hurt riding with him.　60

He once rolled an empty coach and "busted in"　61
his sides. But characteristically, he never saw a doctor　62
about it.　63

Like many men of Gold Rush days, not much　64
was known about Old Charlie's background. A few　65
people heard him talk a bit about running away from　66
a New Hampshire poorhouse at an early age, then　67
working in stables until he began driving stages on the　68
Boston Post Road. His New England twang sup-　69
ported this as his origin.　70

One dark evening on a run, author J. Ross Browne, delighted that he could ride on the box with the famous whip, asked, "How in the world can you see your way?" 71 72 73 74

"Smell it," Charlie said. "Fact is, I've traveled over these mountains so often I can tell where the road is by the sound of the wheels. When they rattle, I'm on hard ground. When they don't rattle, I genr'ly look over the side to see where she's going." 75 76 77 78 79

For a man who knew the animals so well, it was ironic that a kick from a mean horse cost Old Charlie the sight of one eye and caused his retirement from stagecoach driving. He next operated a combination 80 81 82 83 stage station and saloon. Then he went into the cattle business but his sciatic rheumatism—the bane of coach drivers—forced his retirement. He moved to a small place near Watsonville, California, where his neighbors and their children helped make his final years happy. He died on December 29, 1879. 84 85 86 87 88 89

His friends brought his best outfit out of mothballs and prepared to outfit him in the style in which they were sure he would have liked to depart. 90 91 92

It was then they discovered Mr. Charles D. Parkhurst, the wiry Concord driver who never flinched at danger, had a secret. Old Charlie was a woman. 93 94 95 96

Source: "Charlie Parkhurst: The Stagecoach Driver with a Secret," *PG & E Progress,* Pacific Gas and Electric Company. Reprinted by permission of the publisher.

Postreading Activities
CHARLIE PARKHURST: THE STAGECOACH DRIVER WITH A SECRET

Part A CHECKING YOUR PREDICTIONS. Charlie's secret was that he was actually a woman. Did you guess "his" secret before you read the story?

Part B REMEMBERING FACTS. Answer the following questions by writing "T" for "true" or "F" for "false" on a separate piece of paper. Rewrite each false statement to make it a true statement. Try to answer without looking back at the story.

T F 1. Charlie worked as a stagecoach driver during the goldrush days.

T F 2. The first time Charlie was held up, he successfully fought off the highwaymen.

T F 3. Charlie's career lasted about 30 years.

T F 4. Charlie was extremely tall.

T F 5. Charlie usually talked a great deal.

T F 6. The "Concord," mentioned in the story, is a type of shotgun.

T F 7. Charlie never drank whiskey.

T   F   8.   When he was young, Charlie ran away from a poorhouse in New Hampshire.

T   F   9.   Charlie retired as a driver because he developed rheumatism.

T   F 10.   Charlie died in 1979.

Part C FOLLOWING STRUCTURE.   Asnwer the following questions on a separate piece of paper. You may go back to the story.

11.   What are "those words" (line 5)?

12.   What are "the others" (line 12)?

13.   What is "the bank" (line 52)?

14.   Who is the "famous whip" (line 73)?

15.   Who are "they" (line 77)?

16.   Who are "they" (line 93)?

17.   What is the full name of the "driver" (line 94)?

Part D IDENTIFYING MAIN IDEAS.   Answer each question by selecting the best choice. You may refer to the story.

18.   Which of the following best expresses the main idea of the paragraph that begins on line 34?

    A.   Highwaymen were a real source of danger to stagecoach drivers.

    B.   Bad roads were more of a problem than highwaymen.

    C.   The roads were covered with poles and brush.

19.   Which of the following best expresses the main idea of the paragraph that begins on line 47?

    A.   Charlie's quick action saved the coach from falling into the river.

    B.   There were many old bridges on the roads Charlie traveled.

    C.   Passengers were grageful that they were riding with Charlie Parkhurst as the driver.

Part E DISCUSSING YOUR REACTIONS AND INSIGHTS.   Consider these questions for possible discussion in the classroom.

20.   Name several things you would or would not like if you had Charlie's job.

21.   Do you think that Charlie would have had the same degree of success as a driver if everyone knew that he was really a woman? Why?

Prereading Activities
NOT PRETTY AT ANY SPEED:
BEING AN INSPECTOR AT A CHICKEN-CUTTING PLANT

Part A MAKING PREDICTIONS.   You will be reading a story that has the title given above. Predict one or two specific things an inspector looks for when he or she examines chickens being prepared for market.

Part B UNDERSTANDING NEW WORDS.   Below are words used in the story you are about to read. List them on a separate piece of paper. To the right of each, write its meaning, selecting from the scrambled list.

Word
1. decibel
2. entrails
3. carcass
4. shackles
5. postmortem
6. tedious
7. contamination
8. peruse

Meaning (listed in scrambled order)
A. internal organs of an animal, es- pecially intestines
B. unit of measurement for determining the loudness of sound
C. the dead body of an animal
D. an examination, usually shortly after death
E. tiresome or uninteresting, monotonous
F. metal fastenings put on wrists or legs to hold or restrain
G. impurity caused by contact, usually with a poisonous substance
H. to examine, usually with great care

Complete each of the following sentences by writing one of the preceding words in the blank. The sentences are not part of the story but are given to help you understand the new words. (Do NOT write on this page. Rewrite the sentences on a separate piece of paper.)

9.   Be sure to remove the _____ before roasting the chicken.

10.   We don't know the exact _____ level, but we know that the noise was so loud it hurt our ears.

11.   Because the job was very repetitive, he found it to be _____ .

12.   When you buy used clothing, you should _____ it very careful- ly since it is sold "as is."

13. The veterinarian performed a _____ examination on the dead cow.

14. Slaves were often restrained with _____ .

15. She called the SPCA to report that the _____ of a large animal was in the middle of the highway.

16. When large numbers of people started to get sick, we first suspected _____ of the water supply.

Part C FOCUSING YOUR READING. Now read the story. While you read, think about what you personally would and would not like about the job of inspector at a chicken-cutting plant.

NOT PRETTY AT ANY SPEED
Being an Inspector at a Chicken-Cutting Plant

Hurlock, MD

Inspector Sylvester Blake sat in a 90-decibel roar, in a drizzle of blood and flying entrails, and watched perhaps his 20,000th chicken carcass of the day go by at the rate of 70 per minute.

They hung from shackles, by their ankles. Blake tapped each one rhythmically with a stainless steel wand as it crossed in front of his face.

Blake and five fellow inspectors for the Department of Agriculture are the federal presence in this chicken "factory" on Maryland's Eastern Shore, one of two factories that process 50 million chickens a year for Bayshore Foods, Inc. under the Shorgood label.

It is only a mid-sized plant in an industry that turns out more than 10 billion pounds of chicken flesh a year nationwide.

For the last 20 years, by law, the USDA inspectors have been posted at plants such as this one to make postmortem checks of each bird and certify them disease-free and "wholesome" before their last ride to somebody's dinner table.

But this summer, some of the 2,200 slaughter inspectors squawked about a change in their procedures, ordered by the USDA, to speed up the flow of fowl.

Watching the birds go by at up to 70 birds a minute (the new national maximum), some are complaining about an assembly line affliction called "line hypnosis." They lose awareness and concentration. The birds become just a blurred yellow vision, they say, and some bad ones may slip through.

Agriculture officials counter that the speedup—as much as 30 percent higher in some cases—was a long-needed effort to improve government efficiency. They say USDA inspectors were actually a drag on an industry churning out one of today's rare supermarket bargains.

In one of the government's most physically tedious occupations, the inspectors have been using the same procedure for 20 years—a hands-on postmortem of each bird, inside and out, searching for bruises, breast blisters, chicken cancer, and contamination.

The line speeds varied from region to region, some as low as 54 birds per minute. In any case, several inspectors on a line divided up the birds so that no single person was responsible for all of them.

Now, each inspector has less bird to cover but more birds to check—and that, they say, is the problem.

Just minutes before they pass inspection, the noisy, distraught birds are snatched from

their coops by men called hangers and strung 59
up in shackles by their ankles. One machine 60
cuts their throats and another strips and 61
dumps their feathers into a smelly, damp 62
heap on a steaming floor. 63

At the first check point, one inspector 64
peruses the outside of every bird, with the 65
help of a long mirror that reflects its backside. 66

Down the line, a machine and several 67
women employees pull the bird's viscera out 68
of the body cavity, draping it in an almost 69
ceremonial "presentation" for Uncle Sam's 70
representatives. Two more inspectors divide 71
up the chore of checking the little organs and 72
the cavity, each probing every second bird 73
quickly with their fingers. 74

At an unspoken signal—a nod or gesture— 75
from the inspector, a trimmer standing nearby 76
cuts away the bad sections of bird. Borderline 77
cases are decided by the chief inspector, a 78
veterinarian. 79

"It (the new system) is here, so I've got to 80
live with it," said Dr. Donald Noll, the vet- 81
inspector at the Hurlock plant. He said he has 82
been in the business for 30 years. Inspectors 83
are coping with the threat of line hypnosis, as 84
plant employees do, he said, by rotating to 85
different spots periodically. The inspectors 86
still have the authority to slow down the line 87
if the bad birds start to pile up and they get 88
behind. 89

Blake, an inspector for 16 months, doesn't 90
mind the change so much. "I really love this 91
job," he said. "I could have still been a truck 92
driver. It gets monotonous sometimes for 93
inspectors or anybody who works in here," 94
Blake said. "But you just don't let it. You sit 95
down, then stand up, shift your weight, any- 96
thing. Or like I do, to kind of get the rhythm 97
of the line, I tap the bird." 98

The plant workers wear earplugs against 99
the roar, hardhats to protect them from fall- 100
ing chickens, nose masks where there is dust 101
and feathers, rain slicks and plastic boots 102
against the grease and blood and metal 103
gloves to keep from slicing fingers off with 104
knives and bone breakers. 105

At any speed, the chicken-processing 106
business is not pretty. 107

The inspectors who oppose the new sys- 108
tem argue that public health is being en- 109
dangered. 110

"There's going to be a scandal," said Jim 111
Murphy, president of the National Joint Coun- 112
cil of Food Inspection locals, under the Ameri- 113
can Federation of Government Employees. 114
"This is a very competitive business, and the 115
changes amount to the companies doing 116
voluntary quality control." 117

Union spokespeople also said that in 118
addition to line hypnosis and eye strain, 119
inspectors occasionally had to contend with 120
bribe attempts by packers and that a few of 121
the less sturdy inspectors ended up in jail. 122

But officials of the USDA and the broiler 123
industry say the real problem is the union's 124
concern that the change will rob it of poten- 125
tial members, plus a resistance to any change 126
by older employees, many of whom have 127
been eyeballing chickens for 20 years. 128

"The way the industry is growing, if they 129
kept the old system, they'd have to add thou- 130
sands of inspectors to the federal payroll," 131
said William P. Roenigk of the National Broiler 132
Council, which represents the industry. 133

Inspectors last year condemned as "bad" 134
about two percent of the young chickens 135
they inspected, down from four percent 20 136
years ago, officials said. But that two percent 137
still amounts to around 200 million pounds of 138
chicken. 139

Source: Kathy Sawyer, "Not Pretty at Any Speed," *The Washington Post*, 1979. Reprinted by permission of the publisher.

Postreading Activities
NOT PRETTY AT ANY SPEED:
BEING AN INSPECTOR AT A CHICKEN-CUTTING PLANT

Part A CHECKING YOUR PREDICTIONS. The answer to Part A of the *Prereading Activities* is that an inspector specifically looks for bruises, breast blisters, chicken cancer, and contamination.

Were any of your predictions on the right track?

Part B REMEMBERING FACTS. Answer the following questions by selecting the best choice for each. Try to answer without looking back at the story.

1. At what rate do the chickens go by an inspector?

   A. 5 per minute   B. 70 per minute   C. 150 per minute

2. The USDA recently ordered that the rate the chickens go by inspectors should be

   A. increased.   B. decreased.   C. kept the same.

3. According to the author, at the supermarket, chicken is

   A. overpriced.   B. a bargain.   C. about average.

4. The workers who take the chickens from their coops and string them up are called

   A. "vets."   B. "inspectors."   C. "hangers."

5. What is done if much of a chicken is good, but it has a bad section?

   A. The section is cut away.

   B. The whole chicken is thrown away.

   C. The bad section is treated with a chemical to make it good.

6. How does Inspector Blake feel about his job?

   A. He dislikes it.   B. He thinks it's okay.   C. He loves it.

7. What percent of chickens were condemned as "bad" last year?

   A. 2%   B. 12%   C. 20%

Part C SCANNING FOR INFORMATION. Quickly scan the story to locate the paragraphs in which the following information is given. On a separate piece of paper identify each paragraph by writing the number of the line in which the paragraph begins.

8. Which paragraph tells how many pounds of chicken are produced nationally each year?

9. Which paragraph tells how many years inspectors have been using the same procedure?

10. Which paragraph gives the opinion of Dr. Noll on the new system?

11. Which paragraph names the protective clothing worn by the plant workers?

12. Which paragraph tells how many pounds of chicken are condemned as "bad" each year?

Part D DRAWING INFERENCES.   Use everyday reasoning skills to answer the following questions.

13. For what words does "USDA" (line 19) probably stand?

14. Why do inspectors probably use mirrors (line 66) to see the backsides of chickens instead of directly looking at the backsides?

15. Why do inspectors probably use "an unspoken signal" (line 75) instead of words to communicate?

16. What type of "scandal" (line 111) is probably being referred to?

17. Why do inspectors sometimes have to contend with bribe attempts (line 121)

Part E DISCUSSING YOUR REACTIONS AND INSIGHTS.   Consider these questions for possible discussion in the classroom.

18. Describe what you personally would and would not like about the job of inspector at a chicken cutting plant. Include your reasons.

19. Do you think it was right for the government to order a speed up of the inspection process? Why?

20. Even though chickens are inspected by the government, do you still need to be careful when selecting a chicken while shopping at a market? Why?

Prereading Activities
ANDREW HALLIDIE—THE CANNY CABLE CAR INVENTOR

Part A MAKING PREDICTIONS.   You will be reading a true story that has the title given above. Using the information in the title and any hunches you may have, answer each question with a "yes" or "no."

1. Was it easy to invent and build the first cable car system?

2. Did San Francisco probably already have a system for transporting up and down steep hills?

Part B UNDERSTANDING NEW WORDS.   Find the following words in the story in the lines listed below. Do not read the whole story yet, just the paragraph in which each word appears. Try to determine the meanings of the words from the context. List the words on a separate piece of paper and define each.

3. immigrant (line 7)
4. gruesome (23)
5. conveyance (line 27-28)
6. undaunted (line 35)

7. tenacious (line 42)
8. franchise (line 46)
9. posh (line 71)
10. inimitable (line 82)

Part C FOCUSING YOUR READING.   Now read the entire story. While you read, think about whether Andrew Hallidie deserves an important place in the history of San Francisco.

ANDREW HALLIDIE—
THE CANNY CABLE CAR INVENTOR

California

The idea was impossible, people said. No 1
one had ever built a system that could haul 2
vehicles up and lower them down hills as steep 3
as San Francisco's. 4

But Andrew S. Hallidie was convinced he 5
had the answer: a cable car. 6

An immigrant Scot, Hallidie was already 7
known in the city and mining camps for the 8
manufacture of fine quality wire rope, and for his 9
love of adventure. 10

Legend has it that his idea gripped him on a 11
rainy winter evening in 1869. As he watched an 12
overloaded horse-drawn streetcar struggle up a 13
hill, one of the horses slipped on the slick 14
cobblestones—a not uncommon occurrence. The 15
driver slammed the car brake lever with such 16
force that the chain mechanism snapped. 17

At once the car began to slide downhill, 18
dragging the horses over the pavement. When 19
the car came to rest at the bottom, the terrified 20
passengers clambered out. The horses were 21
dead. 22

Shocked by the gruesome accident, Hallidie 23
recalled the cruel treatment often inflicted on 24
horses that hauled the street cars in America 25
and in London where his Scottish parents lived 26
when he was born. He vowed to invent a con- 27
veyance that could operate without horses. 28

By 1871 he had designed a system of mov- 29
ing underground cables which could be gripped 30
and released at will by cars running along tracks 31
in the street. 32

But when he tried to interest investors, 33
they laughed. 34

Undaunted, he finally persuaded three friends 35
to help him share the costs. Then Hallidie 36
plunged into an incredible invention/manufac- 37
turing/construction tour de force. When a new 38
part of apparatus was needed, he invented it. 39
Patterns were created, equipment fabricated. 40
Problems cropped up nearly every day and the 41
tenacious Hallidie would labor into the night 42
solving them. 43

Work continued on "Hallidie's folly," as 44
people were calling it, up to August 1, 1873, the 45
day his street railway franchise was due to 46
expire. Just after midnight, a tired handful of 47
men gathered at the powerhouse, watching and 48
helping workmen until at 5 a.m., Hallidie called 49
for a test. 50

"Jimmie," said Hallidie, turning to one of 51
his most capable employees, "are you ready?" 52

The young man looked down to the bottom 53
of the hill, which was lost in swirls of fog, and 54
backed off, shaking his head. Hallidie quickly 55
shooed the six men on board the car, and 56
released the brake himself. The car descended 57
at 8 miles per hour, with a couple of rest stops 58
along the way. 59

That afternoon, following a hurried exten- 60
sion of the cable line, Mayor William Alvord 61
joined other city officials and a large throng 62
gathered for the official trial run. The cable car 63
was designed to carry 26 people. About 90 64
rushed on board, counting those who ended up 65
on the roof. Except for a short delay above 66
Powell street, the trip went smoothly. 67

The cable car quickly became a financial 68

success and new lines were built. With hills no **69** found the Mechanics Institute and was an **76** longer a travel barrier, vacant sand-covered hill- **70** enthusiastic participant in community affairs. **77** tops soon blossomed with posh apartment **71** To this day, his invention remains a symbol **78** houses and luxurious hotels in the real estate **72** of San Francisco known throughout the world, **79** boom that followed. **73** and the cable cars, despite some problems of **80**

Hallidie served for years as chairman of the **74** aging, still transport residents and tourists in an **81** University of California finance committee, helped **75** inimitable way. **82**

Source: "Andrew Hallidie: The Canny Cable Car Inventor," *PG & E Progress,* Pacific Gas and Electric Company. Reprinted by permission of the publisher.

Postreading Activities
ANDREW HALLIDIE—THE CANNY CABLE CAR INVENTOR

Part A CHECKING YOUR PREDICTIONS. These are the answers to Part A of the *Prereading Activities:* 1. no, 2. yes.

Which of your predictions were correct?

Part B REMEMBERING FACTS. Answer the following questions by writing "T" for "true" or "F" for "false" on a separate piece of paper. Rewrite each false statement to make it a true statement. Try to answer without looking back at the story.

T F 1. Hallidie was born in London.

T F 2. Before cable cars were invented, horses were used to draw streetcars up hills.

T F 3. The cables were placed underground.

T F 4. Hallidie paid for the entire project himself.

T F 5. On the first run, the cable car ran at 55 miles per hour.

T F 6. After it was in operation, the cable car system lost money for a long time.

T F 7. Hallidie was active in other community affairs.

Part C FOLLOWING STRUCTURE. Answer the following questions on a separate piece of paper. You may go back to the story.

8. What is the name of "the city" (line 8)?

9. Who are "they" (line 34)?

10. What is "it" (line 39)?

11. To what does "them" (line 43) refer?

12. To what does "lines" (line 69) refer?

13. To what does "invention" (line 78) refer?

Part D IDENTIFYING THE SEQUENCE OF EVENTS. Below are some events from the story. On a separate piece of paper, list the numbers. To the right of the number of the event that occurred first, write "A." To the right of the second one, write "B," etc. Try to answer without referring to the story.

14. Hallidie moved to the United States.

15. Hallidie talked some friends into helping to pay the costs for inventing the cable car.

16. Hallidie saw some horses killed in an accident.

17. Hallidie took a small number of men on a test ride on a cable car.

18. The mayor attended an official gathering for the trial run.

Part E DISCUSSING YOUR REACTIONS AND INSIGHTS. Consider these questions for possible discussion in the classroom.

19. Do you think that Hallidie deserves an important place in the history of San Francisco? Why?

20. What are some reasons why inventors often have trouble getting people to support their efforts?

21. Why do you think that San Francisco maintains a cable car system even though modern buses might be cheaper and safer to run?

22. Why do you think that Hallidie continued working even though he was laughed at and his invention was called "Hallidie's Folly"?

Prereading Activities
JULIA MORGAN: THE ARCHITECT BEHIND THE CASTLE

Part A MAKING PREDICTIONS. You will be reading a story that has the title given above. Julia Morgan worked in the early part of this century. Speculate on whether men or women first supported her efforts to begin an architectural design business. Explain your answer.

Part B UNDERSTANDING NEW WORDS. Below are words used in the story you are about to read. List them on a separate piece of paper. To the right of each, write its meaning, selecting from the scrambled list.

Word	Meaning (listed in scrambled order)
1. incredulity	A. a statement of belief
2. credo	B. a person who supports others, often the others are artists
3. unobtrusive	
4. rustic	C. to avoid deliberately
5. anomaly	D. simple, unsophisticated
6. relegated	E. disbelief
7. patron	F. not readily noticeable
8. shun	G. assigned to a particular class or position, often a lower position than desired
9. instill	
10. gandiose	H. characterized by greatness in size or intent
11. exhilarating	I. invigorating, stimulating
	J. gradually introduce or implant
	K. deviation from the normal or usual

Complete each of the following sentences by substituting one of the preceding words for the blank. The sentences are not part of the story but are given to help you understand the new words. Do NOT write on this page. Rewrite the sentences on a separate piece of paper.

12. Since she wanted to be _____ , she wore a dark dress.

13. In the past, women were often _____ to certain lower-paying jobs.

14. He worked long hours each day because his _____ was that "success is the result of hard work."

15. The lived in a _____ little cabin in the woods.

16. Because it was a close championship game, we found that watching it was very _____ .

17. His _____ scheme was so complicated that it had no chance of success.

18. She was a good manager because she could _____ a sense of pride into her employees.

19. Because she was very busy, she decided to _____ all new projects.

20. While he silently listened to the lie, his face showed his _____

21. Without the support of his _____ , the artist would have abandoned his career as an artist for lack of sufficient income.

22. Considering that she usually painted tiny portraits, her gigantic, abstract painting was regarded by critics as an _____ .

Part C FOCUSING YOUR READING. Now read the story. While you read, think about how you personally would feel if you were talented in some field yet were discriminated against in that field solely because of your sex.

JULIA MORGAN:
THE ARCHITECT BEHIND THE CASTLE

Architects who knew Julia Morgan's work 1
reacted with incredulity when visiting the 2
Hearst Castle near San Simeon, California as it 3
grew during the '20s and '30s. 4

What shocked and puzzled architects 5
confronted by this vast, ornate structure, was 6
the drastic departure from her credo, "Build- 7
ings should be unobtrusive elements on a 8
landscape." 9

In the years since she opened her own 10
office in 1905, Julia Morgan had gained recog- 11
nition for her tastefully understated homes 12
and buildings that made practical use of 13
wood, rough-cut stones and other rustic 14
materials. This approach plus 14-hour days, 15
six days a week, soon built a thriving business. 16

Why, then, the architectural anomaly 17
near San Simeon. 18

A glimpse at her background and the 19
time suggests some possible answers. Julia 20
Morgan was born in San Francisco in 1872 and 21
was the first woman to graduate from the 22
University of California's College of Civil 23
Engineering. Later she was the first woman 24
architectural graduate of a prestigious school 25
in Paris. At the time she opened her own 26
office, women in the architectural field were 27
relegated, at best, to interior design. 28

Julia Morgan fought this prejudice, quietly 29
and with surprising success, by the quality of 30
her work. 31

"Being female has no bearing on my abili- 32
ty as a designer," she said. 33

She early won support from other women. 34
Her first commission was for Mills College 35
and for the next decade she designed struc- 36
tures for this eminent women's school. She 37

also handled assignments for the YWCA and 38
other organizations run largely by women. 39

Philanthropist Phoebe Hearst appreciated 40
Morgan's work and soon she and her son, the 41
noted publisher William Randolph Hearst, 42
came to be patrons of the spirited young 43
architect. 44

It was an era of rapid growth for the San 45
Francisco area and Morgan's staff grew to 46
about a dozen people. Although she shunned 47
publicity, new commissions kept coming in, a 48
number of them from University of California 49
faculty members who appreciated the warmth 50
and inviting quality of her designs. Even after 51
her reputation was established, she continued 52
to accept small commissions and her practi- 53
cality saved many a homeowner money. 54
More than 600 of her structures were built in 55
the East Bay alone, but most of these burned 56
in a 1923 fire in Berkeley. 57

Julia Morgan's training and experience 58
instilled in her the conviction that the archi- 59
tect's responsibility is to serve the client. This 60
belief was to influence her on the Hearst 61
Castle. 62

It actually started as a simple idea in 1919. 63

"We'll build a small cluster of buildings 64
where my friends can come and enjoy my 65
collection," Hearst told Morgan. 66

The modest cluster grew steadily into 67
what came to be called, with some reason, a 68
"castle." The publisher redrew plans, ex- 69
panded, had walls torn down and rebuilt 70
again. 71

It wasn't the money that kept her return- 72
ing to the job, incorporating each gradiose 73
idea Hearst dreamed up. She admired him as 74

an individual, says biographer Richard W. 75
Longstreth. That plus the duty to serve the 76
client called her back. 77

    Caught up in the exhilarating but often 78
frustrating role of commander of a small army 79
of artisans, Julia Morgan spent an in- 80
creasing amount of time at the site until work 81

was finally halted in 1937. 82

    Today Julia Morgan is best remembered 83
as architect of the Hearst Castle. And the 84
castle, so uncharacteristic of her other work, 85
has become one of the favorite tourist attrac- 86
tions in a state with more than its share of 87
attractions. 88

Source: "Julia Morgan: The Architect Behind the Castle," *PG & E Progress,* June 1981. Reprinted by permission of the publisher.

Postreading Activities
JULIA MORGAN: THE ARCHITECT BEHIND THE CASTLE

Part A CHECKING YOUR PREDICTIONS. The answer to Part A of the *Prereading Activities* is that women (women's organizations) first supported Julia Morgan's activities as an architect.

Part B REMEMBERING FACTS. Answer the questions on a separate piece of paper. Try to answer without looking back at the story.

1. During what decades was the Hearst Castle built?

2. How many hours a day did Julia work while establishing her business?

3. Julia was the first woman architectural graduate of a prestigious school located in what European city?

4. For whom was Julia's first commission as an architect?

5. What happened to most of the 600 structures Julia designed for the East Bay area?

6. Did Julia realize that she'd end up designing a "castle" for Hearst when she first began working for him?

7. In what state was the castle built?

8. Is Julia better remembered for the 600 houses or for the castle?

Part C IDENTIFYING THE SEQUENCE OF EVENTS. Below are some events from the story. On a separate piece of paper, list the numbers. To the right of the number of the event that occurred first, write "A." To the right of the second one, write "B," etc. Try to answer without referring to the story.

9. Julia received a commission from Mills College.

10. Julia graduated from University of California.

11. Julia began to design what would become the Hearst Castle.

12. Julia graduated from a school in Europe.

13. Julia received an assignment from the YWCA.

Part D IDENTIFYING MAIN IDEAS. Answer each question by selecting the best choice. You may go back to the story.

14. Which of the following best expresses the main idea of the paragraph that begins on line 10?

   A. Because of her good ideas and hard work, Julia gained recognition.

   B. Julia worked 14 hours a day for six days each week to get her business started.

   C. Julia liked to design homes out of wood and rough-cut stones.

15. Which of the following best expresses the main idea of the paragraph that begins on line 34?

   A. Julia's first commission was from a women's college.

   B. Julia's early support came from women and women's organizations.

   C. Julia preferred to work for women who appreciated her work.

16. Which of the following best expresses the main idea of the paragraph that begins on line 72?

   A. Julia was not very interested in earning money since she had already earned a lot from earlier commissions.

   B. Julia was willing to keep working for Hearst for years because she admired him and felt a sense of duty.

   C. Richard W. Longstreth was a biographer whose work gave insights into the relationship between Julia and Hearst.

17. Which of the following best expresses the main idea of the paragraph that begins on line 83?

116

A. Hearst Castle is uncharacteristic of Julia's other work.

B. California has more than its share of tourist attractions.

C. Julia is best remembered as architect of Hearst Castle.

Part E DISCUSSING YOUR REACTIONS AND INSIGHTS.   Consider these questions for possible discussion in the classroom.

18. How would you personally feel if you were talented in some field yet were discriminated against because of your sex?

19. Do you personally think that it is right for one man to spend a very great deal of money building a castle instead of using the money to help people in need? Explain.

Prereading Activities
THE GIANTS ARE GOING HOME

Part A MAKING PREDICTIONS. You will be reading a true story that has the title given above. The "giants" are animals that live in the ocean. Use your hunches to predict what type of animal you will be reading about.

Part B UNDERSTANDING NEW WORDS. Find the following words in the story in the lines listed below. Do not read the entire story yet, just the paragraph in which each word appears. Try to determine the meanings of the words from the context. List the words on a separate piece of paper and define each.

1. elusive (line 3)
2. leviathans (line 4)
3. esoteric (line 16)
4. requisites (line 17)
5. courting (line 24)

6. vie (line 26)
7. delinquents (line 32)
8. expeditions (line 37)
9. inevitable (line 59)
10. exuberance (line 70)

Part C FOCUSING YOUR READING. Now read the entire story. While you read, think about whether you would personally like to "watch the giants" and why.

THE GIANTS ARE GOING HOME

It's that time of year when rain-soaked, cold whale lovers gather on windswept points or slippery boat decks in hope of catching a glimpse of the elusive leviathans.

The California Gray Whale migration is impressive. It is the longest journey regularly undertaken by any animal—7,000 miles each way, each year. Twice almost destroyed by whalers greedy for their oil, the grays came under protection in 1943 in the U.S. and Mexico. It is an environmental success story—for now. Some 17,000 of the magnificent animals are currently alive, well and breeding. The major concern now is that if offshore oil drilling should result in a spill during migration, the whales could starve to death.

Whale watching is an art, but not an esoteric one. Its primary requisites are persistence and waterproof clothes. The migration usually begins in late December and lasts until late March when it changes direction and the first whales that went south start heading north again. The migration comes in three waves: first, the pregnant females make their way to the lagoons of Mexico where they give birth, then the courting adults come by, usually in threes, two males to a female since half the females are already south, (the males vie for the females' attention, showing off in all sorts of ways, each hoping he'll be chosen when they finally get to Mexico), and last, the whales that are too young to breed. Many of them don't make it all the way down and hang around off the California coast playing and eating until the grownups come by and chase the young delinquents back north. This year the entire migration began late due to a later than usual ice formation in the north that triggers the urge to head for warmer waters.

One way to spot the whales is to go out on one of the many whale boat expeditions. Some of the less experienced skippers have been charged with being over-eager and interfering with the migration. This is not so of the Merry Jane, Captain Bob Hanlon's boat that leaves Bodega Bay, California. The trips are sponsored by the Marine Mammal Center. Naturalist Ken Minasian accompanies each boatload of enthusiasts. The trip lasts about three hours, and is helped along by a spotter on land at Bodega Head. Dress warmly and in waterproof clothing. It can get a little rough off the Head from time to time. If it's too rough or wet, the trips are canceled and rain checks are issued. The cost is $20.

Another favorite whale watching spot that almost always produces results is Point Reyes Lighthouse in California. Visitors must descend (and later ascend) a flight of steps some thirty stories long (there are rest stops). The point juts so far into the sea that the whales come close enough so that their barnacles can be clearly seen with the naked eye. The animals frequently "spy hop" as they round the bend. Spy hopping involves bobbing up and down vertically with their heads out of water. With the inevitable cheering crowd on shore applauding them, the whales look like hams taking a bow before resuming their journey.

But if you can't do either of the above, simply take a thermos of tea or coffee to some spot along the coast and watch patiently. Look for the telltale spout that signals the whales' presence. You may see them "fluke" when they flip their tails above water jauntily, or if you are very fortunate, you may see one breach—leap up high out of water. They are suspected of breaching out of sheer exuberance.

At worst you will not see a whale, but will **71** watch the waves crash in, the gulls battle the wind, **72** the ducks bobbing merrily in the swells. Even **73** unsuccessful whalewatching has its rewards. **74**

Source: Andrea Granahan, "The Giants are Going Home," *The Paper,* 1983. Reprinted by permission of the publisher.

Postreading Activities
THE GIANTS ARE GOING HOME

Part A CHECKING YOUR PREDICTIONS. The "giants" are whales. Was your prediction correct?

Part B REMEMBERING FACTS. Answer the questions on a separate piece of paper. Try to answer without looking back at the story.

1. What is the specific name of the particular type of whale discussed in the story?

2. What did whalers want from the whales?

3. About how many of the particular type of whales are now alive?

4. When does the migration usually begin?

5. What is special about the whales who first head south to Mexico?

6. How much does a whale-watching trip on the Merry Jane cost?

7. What is "spy hopping"?

8. What does "fluke" mean?

9. Why does the author say that "Even unsuccessful whalewatching has its rewards."?

Part C FOLLOWING STRUCTURE. Answer the following questions on a separate piece of paper. You may go back to the story.

10. To what does "it" (line 6) refer?

11. To what does "one" (line 17) refer?

12. To what does "it" (line 19) refer?

13. Whose "heads" are referred to in line 59?

Part D IDENTIFYING THE AUTHOR'S TONE. Write the numbers of the following items on a separate piece of paper. Identify how you think the author feels about each by writing "good" or "bad" for each. Use the context of the story to identify the answers.

14. whale watching

15. the California Gray Whale

16. the whalers mentioned in the story

17. naturalist Ken Minasian

18. "breaching" by whales

Part E DISCUSSING YOUR REACTIONS AND INSIGHTS. Consider these questions for possible discussion.

19. Do you think you would personally like to go on a whalewatching expedition? Give several reasons for your answer.

20. Do you think it's right for the government to try to protect the California Gray Whale from the whalers? Why?

Prereading Activities
IDIOT SAVANT:
THE EXTRAORDINARY SCULPTURE OF A RETARDED ARTIST

Part A MAKING PREDICTIONS. The term "idiot savant" in the title above means "learned idiot." It is used to describe someone who is extremely retarded in general but has some highly developed, incredible abilities. Use your hunches to predict the answers to the following questions.

1. Did the artist probably receive his art training at an art college?

2. Do the people who take care of the retarded artist probably encourage his artistic interests?

Part B UNDERSTANDING NEW WORDS. Find the following words in the story in the lines listed below. Do not read the whole story yet, just the paragraph in which each word appears. Try to determine the meanings of the words from the context. List the words on a separate piece of paper and define each.

3. apt (line 19)
4. classic (line 22)
5. manipulating (line 52)
6. uncanny (line 59)

7. robust (line 99)
8. nurture (line 102)
9. exploited (line 141)

Part C FOCUSING YOUR READING. Now read the entire story. While you read, think about whether "idiot savant" is a good term to use to describe the main character.

IDIOT SAVANT:
The Extraordinary Sculpture of a Retarded Artist

Boulder, CO

Alonzo owes almost everything to his art. 1

If not for his talent at hand-sculpting lifelike 2
miniature animals out of wax, Alonzo might not be 3
able to dress himself, brush his teeth or dream of 4
someday owning a horse. 5

Alonzo—his last name is Clemens but everyone 6
simply calls him by his first name—is a 25-year-old 7
retarded man who lives here in a group home for the 8
developmentally disabled. He also has an extraor- 9
dinary talent for wax sculpture that amazes experts in 10
both art and psychology. 11

With an IQ of about 40 and the social skills of a 12
6-year-old—his dark eyes are usually hooded and he 13
often says "Yet" for "Yes"—Alonzo's remarkable 14
sculpting skill classifies him as an "idiot savant." 15

From the French for "learned idiot," the phrase 16
is disdained by mental health professionals because of 17
the connotations of "idiot." But modern psychology 18
has not come up with a more apt term for people who 19
are severely retarded yet have some incredible 20
abilities. 21

"He's a classic example," Richard Ratliff, a 22
Boulder psychologist, says of Alonzo. "Obviously, he 23
has some spectacular skills." 24

Ratliff is a member of the staff at Carmel Ltd., 25
the private group home where Alonzo and 75 other 26
retarded adults eat, sleep and relax when not in 27
vocational training classes or earning paychecks 28
doing simple jobs in the community. 29

Alonzo's work is for sale, and he is often invited 30
to art shows where crowds gather to watch him work. 31
But he only attends two or three shows a year because 32
Carmel cannot afford to have a staff member spend a 33
full day driving him to and from a show and then 34
staying with him to set prices and make change. 35

However, Jim Graves, the administrator at 36
Carmel, welcomes visitors to the large, cheerfully 37
busy group home in a quiet residential area near the 38
Colorado University Campus. 39

There, Alonzo spends much of his time in the 40
third-floor bedroom he shares with another resident. 41
Alonzo semi-slumps in a chair as he works his wax, 42
ignoring the stereo and television. He bought the 43
stereo and TV with money he earned as a stable-boy 44
and from selling his art, and they are both on full blast 45
every waking moment he is home. 46

When Graves introduces a visitor, Alonzo 47
smiles shyly, bobs his beard and extends whichever 48
hand seems more convenient. Shaking hands, one is 49
aware of both softness and strength, and of the 50
warmth coming through the layers of callus from 51
pitching hay and manipulating cold, stiff wax. 52

Will Alonzo show the visitor his work? 53

"Yet," he says, nodding and bobbing the beard 54
again. 55

Ratliff says that while idiots savant are ex- 56
tremely rare, Alonzo is even more rare because his 57
unusual skill is in art. More often, an idiot savant's 58
special gift will be in some sort of uncanny mathe- 59
matical ability, such as doing complicated equations 60
very quickly or automatically naming the day of the 61
week for any date in the last century. 62

A ward of the state of Colorado, Alonzo spent 63
his first 21 years in a state institution where nurses 64
used his passion for sculpting to teach him how to do 65
things like tie his shoes. For making progress in social 66
or hygiene skills, Alonzo was given modeling clay to 67
play with. But if he refused to do something the nurses 68
wanted him to do, the clay was taken away. 69

That form of punishment ended, however, 70
when Alonzo was a teen-ager and tiny little horses, 71
sticky and black, were found under his bed. Alonzo 72
had been sneaking out of his bed in the middle of the 73
night, creeping onto the roof of the institution and 74

making the figures out of tar he scraped away with his 75
fingernails. 76

It was shortly after Alonzo came to Carmel— 77
where it costs the state $32 a day to keep him—that a 78
student volunteer introduced him to microcrystalline 79
wax, which artists buy in thick, hard black or white 80
slabs that look and feel more like marble than wax. 81

Now, Alonzo works almost exclusively in wax. 82
Clay, he says, is "too soft." 83

Using nothing but his hands, Alonzo shapes 84
slivers of wax into horses, cows, elephants, Brahma 85
bulls, buck deer. 86

"Big animals," is what he says, in his thick and 87
often halting speech, when asked to name his favorite 88
thing in the whole world. He sees horses and cows on 89
the ranch on the outskirts of town where he works, 90
but he copies other animals from television and from 91
books. 92

"I asked Alonzo to do some dogs a couple of 93
weeks ago, but his dogs all looked like his cows," says 94
Knox Kinlaw, a Carmel counselor. "So I took him to 95
a store and bought a dog book, and now he does all 96
kinds of dogs perfectly." 97

Alonzo does sculpt humans, too; he recently did 98
a robust, bearded farmer carrying a pail and a radio. 99
But Alonzo's people are not nearly as striking as his 100
animals. 101

"In animals, he finds he can nurture them and 102
take each of them and treat them with great dignity," 103
Ratliff says. 104

When interest is shown in a particular stallion, 105
fat and contented from bossing his mares, Alonzo 106
leans forward. The piece took him two days to make. 107
His eyes grow wide and bright, and he says, carefully, 108
"Half quarter horse. Half Arabian." 109

How much? 110

"Forty dollars," Alonzo says, his smile and eyes 111
widening again. 112

Well, how much for the wildebeest that is barely 113
one fourth the size of the horse and took only an hour 114
to make? 115

"Thirty-nine," Alonzo says. 116

"He has trouble with money," Graves says with 117
no apparent concern. He actually sets Alonzo's pri- 118
ces, usually $20-$30 for the big pieces and $5-$10 for 119
the smaller ones. 120

Alonzo doesn't know exactly what money is 121
worth, but he knows it can buy him a TV, a stereo and 123
maybe someday his own horse. He also knows it can 124
buy him more wax, so now he saves his figures 125
instead of showing them to his friends and then 126
flattening them so he can reuse the microcrystalline. 127

Much of Alonzo's allowance of $8 a week is 128
spent on wax. The rest of the roughly $1,500 he 129
makes a year from the ranch and his art sales go into 130
the Carmel savings account that yielded the TV and 131
stereo. 132

Graves and Ratliff would like to see Alonzo 133
become a commercial success, but not just so he can 134
eventually pay his own way at Carmel. 135

"He's intensely proud of his work and the inter- 136
est people show in it," Ratliff says. "It makes us want 137
to provide him the opportunities most handi- 138
capped people do not have." 139

Graves worries that people might think Alonzo 140
is being exploited if Carmel made him a full-time 141
commercial artist rather than a stableboy whose 142
night-time hobby is making models of the horses he 143
grooms by day. 144

At the same time, Graves says, Carmel's philos- 145
ophy is to help residents develop their skills as fully as 146
possible, and art is Alonzo's strongest skill. If he has 147
the potential to make a good living as an artist, should 148
it be denied just because he is retarded? 149

Source: Timothy Harper, "Idiot Savant: The Extraordinary Sculpture of a Retarded Artist," Associated Press, 1983. Reprinted by permission of the publisher.

Postreading Activities
IDIOT SAVANT:
THE EXTRAORDINARY SCULPTURE OF A RETARDED ARTIST

Part A CHECKING YOUR PREDICTIONS.   These are the answers to Part A of the *Prereading Activities:* 1. no, 2. yes.

Which of your predictions were correct?

Part B REMEMBERING FACTS.   Answer the following questions by writing "T" for "true" or "F" for "false" on a separate piece of paper. Rewrite each false statement to make it a true statement. Try to answer without looking back at the story.

T   F   1.   Alonzo has the social skills of a 12-year-old.

T   F   2.   Alonzo attends several dozen art shows a year.

T   F   3.   Alonzo currently lives in Colorado.

T   F   4.   Alonzo's TV and stereo were bought with money he had earned.

T   F   5.   An idiot savant's special skill is more likely to be in math than in art.

T   F   6.   Alonzo now sculpts in wax.

T   F   7.   Alonzo's large pieces usually sell for $20 to $30.

T   F   8.   Alonzo is a full-time commercial artist.

Part C FOLLOWING STRUCTURE.   Answer the following questions on a separate piece of paper. You may go back to the story.

9.   What is the full name of the "he" referred to in line 23?

10.   Whose "eyes" are referred to in line 108?

11.   What is the full name of the "he" referred to in line 118?

12.   To what does the first "it" in line 137 refer?

Part D IDENTIFYING MAIN IDEAS.   Answer each question by selecting the best choice. You may go back to the story.

13. Which of the following best expresses the main idea of the paragraph that begins on line 87?

    A. Big animals are Alonzo's favorite thing.

    B. Alonzo copies some animals from television and books.

    C. Alonzo is personally familiar with horses and cows.

14. Which of the following best expresses the main idea of the paragraph that begins on line 121?

    A. Alonzo has to reuse his wax.

    B. Alonzo has a rough idea of what money can be used for.

    C. Alonzo refuses to show his sculptures to his friends.

Part E DISCUSSING YOUR REACTIONS AND INSIGHTS. Consider these questions for possible discussion in the classroom.

15. Do you think that "idiot savant" is a good term to use to describe people who are like the main character? Why?

16. Do you think it would be exploiting Alonzo to make him into a full-time commercial artist? Explain your reasoning.

Prereading Activities
NEW DELHI IS TALKING ABOUT CHILD MARRIAGE

Part A MAKING PREDICTIONS. You will be reading a true story that has the title given above. Using the information in the title and any hunches you may have, answer each question in a sentence or two.

1. Do all people in India probably favor child marriage?

2. Is child marriage probably a new or old tradition?

Part B UNDERSTANDING NEW WORDS Below are scrambled definitions of words used in the story you are about to read. Unscramble the definitions by rearranging the phrases. Phrases are separated by double dashes (//). Then write a sentence using each word.

3. **delicate** (adjective) careful handling, // needing // tact, etc.

4. **banned** (verb) law // by custom or // prohibited

5. **patronage** (noun) given by a person // support // or group // or encouragement

6. **auspicious** (adjective) of // or luck // suggestive // success // future

7. **oblivious** (adjective) of // forgetful // unaware or // something

8. **illiterate** (adjective) or culture // having // knowledge, experience, // limited

9. **presumably** (adverb) very likely // seeming // probable or

Part C FOCUSING YOUR READING. Now read the story. While you read, think about how you personally feel about child marriage and try to think of one or two reasons for your feeling.

NEW DELHI IS TALKING ABOUT CHILD MARRIAGE

New Delhi, India

The delicate question of child marriage, an age-old custom in India, is again being debated here with charges that the practice is receiving official support in some parts of the country.

In the western desert state of Rajasthan, where mass child marriages take place every year, police have filed charges against a state minister for allowing his 13-year-old daughter to marry.

In the central Indian state of Madhya Pradesh there has been press criticism of the chief minister, Arjun Singh, who recently attended a mass marriage of 87 couples, mostly below the age of 16.

Although marriage under the age of 18 is banned in India, the Indian Express newspaper charged that the Madhya Pradesh weddings took place with the blessing of Singh and his state government which, it said, financed the marriages.

The boys and girls, some aged 11 or 12, were members of the Adivasi tribal or Harijan (untouchable) communities whose parents would not normally be able to afford the festivities that usually go with weddings in India.

In another mass marriage at Wardha village in Madhya Pradesh last month, 55 of the 111 brides were below the age of 10, and one was just 6.

Child marriages have long been common in Madhya Pradesh. The Express said that what was more significant now was that such marriages were taking place under direct official patronage.

In Rajasthan, the mass marriages take place each year on an auspicious day known as Akha Teej.

On this day of the year, Hindus are permitted to perform marriage rites without the supervision of a holy man, who is paid for the function, so poor peasants are able to save money.

Brightly dressed women and children are taken to the marriage ceremonies in long lines of ox carts.

Many of the smaller children sleep through marriage ceremonies totally oblivious of the fact that they have acquired a spouse.

Sometimes as many as 10,000—as was the case in 1979—are married on a single day in Rajasthan.

The Hindustan Times newspaper points out that original legislation against child marriage came into being in India during British rule in 1930.

But it said the fine of 1,000 rupees ($125) for a non-adult male contracting child marriage imposed 50 years ago is unaltered today, though the value of the rupee has decreased perhaps a hundred times.

Punishment for those performing or directing a child marriage, however, had been increased from one month to three months' imprisonment.

The Hindustan Times said there were many loopholes in the law, such as child marriage remaining an offense only if reported within a year. The paper said not a single case under the act had been launched in recent years.

The Tribune newspaper said in an editor- 74 ial: "The illiterate and tradition-bound Indian 75 has continued to ignore the law, and the 76 authorities—presumably finding that the task 77 of enforcing the law is beyond their ca- 78 pacity—look the other way when instances of 79 child marriage are brought to their notice." 80

Source: Granville Watts, "New Delhi is Talking About Child Marriage." Copyright Reuters, 1981. Reprinted by permission of the publisher.

Postreading Activities
NEW DELHI IS TALKING ABOUT CHILD MARRIAGE

Part A CHECKING YOUR PREDICTIONS. These are the answers to Part A of the *Prereading Activities:* 1. No, only some people favor child marriage. 2. Child marriage is probably an old tradition since it was banned in India in 1930. Also, child marriage is referred to as an "age old" custom.

Which of your predictions were correct?

Part B REMEMBERING FACTS. Answer the following questions by selecting the best choice for each. Try to answer without looking back at the story.

1. What position does Arjun Singh hold?

   A. newspaper reporter who is opposed to child marriage

   B. chief minister of an Indian state

   C. a holy man who performs marriage rites

2. According to the writer, are all of the children who get married fully aware of what is happening to them?

   A. yes   B. no   C. The author does not say.

3. A person who performs or directs a child marriage can be imprisoned for how long at the present time?

   A. two weeks   B. three months   C. one year

4. Which of the following is cited as a loophole in the law?

   A. Child marriage is only an offense if reported within a year.

   B. There is a fine of 1,000 rupees for certain offenses.

   C. Child marriages were first banned under British rule.

5. What did one newspaper charge some authorities of doing when instances of child marriage are brought to their attention?

    A. They ignore it.

    B. They write about it.

    C. They make public speeches about it.

Part C SCANNING FOR INFORMATION.   Quickly scan the story to locate the paragraphs in which the following information is given. On a separate piece of paper, identify each paragraph by writing the number of the line in which the paragraph begins.

6. Which is the first paragraph to mention a specific age at which a child was married?

7. Which paragraph mentions that there were 111 brides in a mass marriage?

8. Which paragraph gives the name of the special day for mass marriages in the state of Rajasthan?

9. Which paragraph tells when the original legislation against child marriage was passed?

Part D DISCUSSING YOUR REACTIONS AND INSIGHTS.   Consider these questions for possible discussion in the classroom.

10. How do you personally feel about child marriage? Give one or two reasons for your feelings.

11. Speculate on some reasons why the poor are more likely to allow their young children to become married than are the more affluent.

12. Speculate on some reasons why some government officials seem to be ignoring the law.

13. At what age do you personally think that someone is old enough to be allowed to make a decision about marriage? Explain.

14. What would be your reaction if you were told that you were to be married at an early age to someone you had never met?

Prereading Activities
MAKING PAPER FOR MAKING MONEY

Part A MAKING PREDICTIONS.   You will be reading a true story that has the title given above. Using your hunches, predict whether it is easy to make paper for making money. Also predict whether it would be easy to counterfeit the paper itself without any printing (engraving) on it.

Part B UNDERSTANDING NEW WORDS.   Determine the meaning of each of the following words by reading the sentences in which they appear. Line numbers are given to help you find the sentences. Do *NOT* read the entire story yet. Show your understanding by writing, on a separate piece of paper, the letter of the best meaning for each.

1. sprawling (line 3)

    A. a type of bird whose feathers are used in manufacturing
    B. a type of printing press that prints many sizes of print
    C. spread out in an uneven fashion, taking up more space than needed

2. currency (line 6)

    A. the money, especially paper money, in circulation in a country
    B. the money, especially coins, in circulation in a country
    C. a fruit that is used to get dye for printing

3. expertise (line 11)

    A. an armed guard who protects valuable government property
    B. a type of fable or myth, often humorous
    C. knowledge or skill of someone who has much training in an area

4. specifications (line 48)

    A. permission to do what seems reasonable given current conditions and unforeseen circumstances
    B. nonfiction tales or stories meant to be entertaining
    C. statements regarding particulars such as weight, size, quality, etc.

5. revenues (line 64)

    A. income, usually from a business or business investment
    B. a group of armed guards and their trucks
    C. listings of all items available at a particular time

6. disposable (line 90)

   A. can be printed on
   B. can be used easily
   C. can be thrown away

Part C FOCUSING YOUR READING. Now read the story. While you read, think about whether it is right that only one paper company is given the contracts to make all the paper for the U.S paper money.

MAKING PAPER FOR MAKING MONEY

Dalton, MA

Pity the poor American who can't pull a sample of Crane & Co. paper from his or her pocket.

This sprawling mill complex in the foothills of the Berkshires, owned by the ninth generation of the Crane family, is the sole manufacturer of paper stock for American currency.

The 180-year-old Crane company began making currency stock for the U.S. government in 1879. It had competitors along the way until 1978. That year, Crane & Co. outbid the few other companies in the country that had the expertise to manufacture the paper and became the sole manufacturer of currency stock for the U.S. Bureau of Engraving and Printing.

Although security is tight at the mill where the paper is made and stored, the Massachusetts company is not concerned about would-be counterfeiters learning what materials go into the currency stock.

"There really is no secret," said James Manning, Crane personnel director. "Where counterfeiters would have their problem is getting a supply of raw materials and then having the expertise to make quality paper."

Currency paper is made from cotton and linen rags, which might include remnants of underwear or blue jeans. Added to this are scraps of silk or a synthetic fiber with the same characteristics. Basically, this mixture is cooked, cleaned, bleached and shredded into bits. Somewhere along this process, a vegetable or animal starch is added to hold the mixture together.

The most important ingredient, however, is water. That is why the Crane family went to Dalton, which sits on the banks of the Housatonic River. At the initial stages, when this snow-like material rolls through the line on its way to becoming paper, it is almost 90 percent liquid.

Finally, the mixture is pressed into soggy sheets, wrung, dried and then rolled. Few people, however, including those who have manufactured paper for decades, can turn out the quality product that Crane does.

Manning said the important part of this whole process is the proportions of rag fibers, starch and water.

The paper is checked closely for quality, and sheets that are rejected are ground up and put through the whole process again until they meet the rigid specifications of the Bureau of Engraving.

"Once the paper is taken from the plant, the Bureau of Engraving takes over the security," Manning said.

Few people at Crane know in advance the schedule and routes of the government trucks that transport the paper from the mill to the federal engraving plants, which are located in various parts of the country.

Manning said there has never been a theft of currency paper from Crane, by outsiders or employees, in the company's history.

Crane & Co. would not say how much currency 60
paper is manufactured at the plant. Manning said, 61
however, that the manufacture of currency paper 62
amounts to about 20 percent of its business. Last year, 63
the company had revenues totalling about $80 64
million. 65

The company also supplies Taiwan and "several 66
Latin American countries" with paper for its currency. 67

"We'd be reluctant to say which Latin Ameri- 68
can countries. You can understand that some of them 69
might not want it publicized that their paper currency 70
is manufactured in the United States," Manning said. 71

With one exception, Crane & Co. paper is 100 72
percent rag content. Manning said there are only a 73
dozen manufacturers in the nation that make 100 74
percent rag-content paper. Most paper today is made 75

from wood pulp. 76

Crane & Co. began in 1801 when Zenas Crane 77
established his first paper mill in Dalton. At the time, 78
Thomas Jefferson had taken over the presidency 79
from John Adams, the U.S Constitution was only a 80
dozen years old and only Vermont and Kentucky had 81
been added to the 13 original states. 82

Threatened by fires and economic depressions 83
since its founding, Crane & Co., always led by a 84
family member until the 1975 election of Benjamin 85
Sullivan as its president, proved remarkably adept at 86
survival. 87

After the severe post-Civil War depression, for 88
example, Crane & Co. began manufacturing the 89
disposable paper collar that became the nation's first 90
fashion trend for men. 91

Source: William Cockerham, "Making Paper for Making Money," *The Hartford Courant,* 1981. Reprinted by permission of the publisher.

Postreading Activities
MAKING PAPER FOR MAKING MONEY

Part A CHECKING YOUR PREDICTIONS. These are the answers to the questions in Part A of the *Prereading Activities:* It is difficult to make and counterfeit the paper because it is hard to get the supplies and hard to find the expertise to make quality paper.

Part B REMEMBERING FACTS. Answer the questions on a separate piece of paper. Try to answer without looking back at the story.

1. In what state is the paper manufactured?

2. How old is Crane & Co.?

3. Does the rag content of paper contain more cotton or silk?

4. Why is starch added in the process of making the paper?

5. Has there ever been a theft of the paper from Crane & Co.?

6. Does Crane & Co. make paper only for currency?

7. What is cited as the nation's first fashion trend for men?

Part C SCANNING FOR INFORMATION.   Quickly scan the story to locate the paragraphs in which the following information is given. On a separate piece of paper, identify each paragraph by writing the number of the line in which the paragraph begins.

8. Which paragraph gives the year in which Crane & Co. started making paper for making money?

9. Which paragraph names silk as an ingredient?

10. Which paragraph tells how much income Crane & Co. had last year?

11. Which paragraph gives the first name of the founder of Crane & Co.?

12. Which paragraph tells who took over as president of the company in 1975?

Part D DRAWING INFERENCES.   Use everyday reasoning skills to answer the following questions.

13. What is the probable reason why only few people know in advance the schedule and routes of the government trucks (lines 52-53)?

14. What is the probable reason why some Latin American countries might not want it publicized that their paper for money is made in the United States (lines 68-71)?

15. Has Crane & Co. probably continued to be prosperous even though someone from outside the Crane family has taken over the presidency of the company (lines 85-86)? Explain your reasoning.

Part E DISCUSSING YOUR REACTIONS AND INSIGHTS.   Consider these questions for possible discussion in the classroom.

16. Do you think it is proper that only one company has government contracts to make paper for money even though several companies have the expertise? Why?

17. Which specific fact about making paper for making money did you personally find most interesting? Why?

18. Speculate on the reasons why a paper disposable collar for men became fashionable.

Prereading Activities
MAN RETURNS AFTER 76 DAYS ON RAFT

Part A MAKING PREDICTIONS.   You will be reading a true story that has the title given above. Using the information in the title and any hunches you may have, answer each question in a sentence or two.

1.   Why was the man on a raft instead of a boat or ship?

2.   He only took a very small amount of food with him onto the raft. How did he probably get additional food to eat during the 76 days?

Part B UNDERSTANDING NEW WORDS.   Below are scrambled definitions of words used in the story you are about to read. Unscramble the definitions by rearranging the phrases. Phrases are separated by double slashes (//). Then write a sentence using each word.

3.   **stoically** (adverb) under suffering, // behaving calmly // bad fortune, etc.

4.   **benign** (adjective) good-natured // gentle and

5.   **presumption** (noun) probability of something // evidence that // to the // points

6.   **ordeal** (noun) or trying // any difficult, // experience // painful,

7.   **odyssey** (noun) wandering or // extended // any // journey

8.   **dolphin** (noun) mammals // water-dwelling // with numerous // and often beaklike snout // teeth

Part C FOCUSING YOUR READING.   Now read the story. While reading, assume you are related to the main character. Think about what you would have done while he was missing at sea. Would your behavior be more like that of his wife, brother, or mother?

MAN RETURNS AFTER 76 DAYS ON RAFT

Marlboro, Maine

For weeks the weight of despair mounted, but Frisha Callahan stoically continued her studies at the University of Maine trying with little success to keep her mind off her missing husband.

Steve Callahan, 30, was overdue two months at the West Indies island of Antigua. The boatbuilder and ocean racer from Marlboro had been single-handedly crossing the Atlantic in his 21-foot sloop, *Napoleon Solo*. Callahan designed and built his trim, seaworthy vessel two summers ago, with help from his wife, who is also a seasoned sailor with ocean races to her credit.

"I was getting pretty hopeless. A couple of times I felt like having a nervous breakdown," Frisha recalled, in an interview Saturday at the Callahan home. She gazed toward benign-looking Frenchman Bay, and shuddered. The waiting, the worrying, the inevitable presumption that Steve was lost—was over.

On April 21, local fishermen from the small Caribbean island of Marie-Galante saw sea birds wheeling over something, and perhaps thinking it was a school of fish, shifted course and discovered Steve Callahan in a second-hand rubber raft.

He had drifted for 76 days, over an estimated 2,000 miles of open sea. He had lost 40 pounds from his usual weight of 150, but he was conscious, and after one day in Guadeloupe hospital, he walked out and took a nearby hotel room.

This past Saturday, Frisha spoke with him for the first time since he sailed in early January from the Canary Islands off the northwest coast of Africa. The call fell on the couple's seventh wedding anniversary. Steve sounded remarkably calm. Before coming home, he wanted to pick up his mail in Antigua, a small island east of Puerto Rico. But the quiet-spoken, reserved young mariner was not unmoved by his 2½ month ordeal.

"It's like being born again. I can feel, touch and smell again," Steve told Frisha in their brief phone conversation, marred by a poor connection between Marlboro and Guadeloupe. He did not know exactly when he would return to Maine.

Frisha said many pieces of the puzzle are still missing, and Steve joked on the phone that he has at least two books coming out of his adventure. How did he have enough water to survive? And how did he have enough will to survive?

Steve told a reporter in Guadeloupe that at times he "bawled like a baby," and of course there was no comfort—not for 76 days. When Frisha heard that, when she thought about the intense loneliness and uncertainty, she too cried. Both Frisha and Steve fought despair, and won.

On his 75th night since the surprise sinking of his sloop—he thinks a whale struck her broadside—Steve saw the lights of Guadeloupe, the lights of hope. Incredibly, Steve was only 100 miles off in his calculations of his whereabouts. He used two pencils to create a navigational aid, a cross-staff, and he logged his progress daily in a journal.

Some of the dreariest moments of his

odyssey were sighting ships. Seven vessels 73
passed him; nobody noticed him. 74

Steve told Frisha he was asleep when the 75
whale—or perhaps it was a ship—struck his 76
wooden-hulled boat. She sank so swiftly 77
Steve had only enough time to snatch a few 78
supplies. He stowed in his life raft an inex- 79
pensive speargun, two pints of water, a fish- 80
ing dropline, pencils and his journal, some 81
food, charts, his sleeping bag and, oddly 82
enough, a book about a man in similar 83
straits—who floated at sea for 37 days. Steve 84
does not believe he set a record in his ordeal, 85
but certainly it is a personal record, and an 86
unmatched feat for this Maine man who fol- 87
lows the sea. 88

Rainwater may have helped Steve stay 89
alive, and on day 43 he managed to spear a 90
dolphin that followed him awhile. Then he 91
dried the meat on his raft. But as he hauled 92
the dolphin aboard, he gashed his inflatable 93
raft and it began leaking air. He patched it; it 94
leaked again; he fixed it. Sharks tailed him 95
some days. 96

Frisha, overwhelmed and grateful that 97
her husband has been rescued, does not have 98
those feelings for the U.S. Coast Guard. "The 99
Coast Guard called off the search a month 100

before. I guess they'd closed the file," she 101
said bitterly. 102

Steve's brother, Edd, never gave up hope, 103
however. A Hawaii resident and excellent 104
mariner, Edd contacted all shipping lines that 105
had vessels traveling where Steve could be 106
found. He alerted ports, planes, and anyone 107
he could think of. He called radio stations, 108
and maintained communications between 109
himself and his parents, in the Boston area, 110
and Frisha in Maine. 111

Frisha and Edd both wonder why a spe- 112
cial device aboard Solo, the EPIRB, appar- 113
ently did not function. EPIRB stands for 114
"emergency position indicating radio bea- 115
con." "If it had worked, though, would 116
anyone have picked up its signal?" they 117
wondered. 118

Meanwhile, Steve, as alone as man ever 119
can be, figured a drift chart and his probable 120
course. He knew he wouldn't give in. He 121
knew he was over the Continental shelf when 122
the water color changed. He saw birds, and 123
birds gave him hope. In fact, he managed to 124
catch and eat a couple of birds, Frisha said. 125

"All through it," Frisha learned from the 126
phone call, "Steve kept dreaming he was 127
found, and he was talking to people." He 128
would wake up in the vast, timeless expanse 129
of the Atlantic. The only change was the date 130
in his log. 131

As the days wore on, Frisha said, "Things 132
came back to Steve. Things people said. Like I 133
said to him 'you'll probably drown, but not 134
this trip.' He kept remembering stuff like 135
that." Steve also heard his mother's voice in 136
the wind. She would smile on him and say, 137
"After all I did bringing you into this world, 138
you're not going to get out of it this easily." 139

Sometimes the dreams gave him strength. 140
In fact, his mother was often on the phone 141
with Frisha, in tears. "And now that he's 142
found, she's still in tears," Frisha said good- 143
humoredly. She grew serious again: "I want 144
to see him," she said, and the statement 145
seemed to sum up, simply, the weeks of not 146
knowing. In some ways, his distant rescue 147
hardly seems real. 148

140

When Steve was found, he had his T-shirt, and he made a sort of loincloth. He hadn't even had time to grab his clothes as *Solo* sank. "You needn't worry, I wasn't indecent," he told his mother. (149–153)

Although Steve's voice was calm over the phone, he "sounded like someone who's been through a lot," Frisha said. "He's pretty scrawny." (154–158)

Steve told Frisha that as the days passed, survival seemed increasingly difficult. But when rescued, Steve got up and walked, bronzed but sunken-cheeked. (159–162)

Frisha said she was upset by initial publicity. First there were prying phone calls from daily newspapers. Then the stories that appeared did not seem to give credit to her husband's considerable experience and obvious good seamanship. (163–168)

"Steve is no lunatic. They made him out to be this crazy guy sailing alone," she said. Actually, Frisha has accompanied Steve many times, including a honeymoon sail off Cape Cod in gale force winds. Perhaps it takes a sailor to understand another sailor, she suggested. (169–175)

Frisha said Steve "feels like he's starting life again ... like a child, he sees things with wonder." But unlike a child, "he sounded like he wanted to be more settled." (176–179)

Meanwhile, the people of Marie-Galante Island have treated Steve Callahan with kindness and respect, not to mention admiration. "It's really spiritual," Frisha said. Steve told her, "They feel I was given to them." (180–185)

Source: Steve Cartwright, "Sea Returns Man after 76 Days Alone on Raft in the Sea," *The Ellsworth American* Ellsworth, Maine, 1982. Reprinted by permission of the publisher.

Postreading Activities
MAN RETURNS AFTER 76 DAYS ON RAFT

Part A CHECKING YOUR PREDICTIONS. These are the answers to Part A of the *Prereading Activities:* 1. He was on the raft because his sloop sunk at sea. 2. He got food by catching some birds and a dolphin. Since he took a fishing dropline with him, he may have also caught some other types of fish.

Which of your predictions were on the right track?

Part B REMEMBERING FACTS. Answer the questions on a separate piece of paper. Try to answer without referring to the story.

1. In what state does Frisha live?

2. What was the name of Steve Callahan's sloop?

3. About how many miles did Steve drift at sea in the raft?

4. How many days did Steve spend in the hospital after he was rescued?

5. What does Steve think caused his sloop to sink?

6. Was Frisha grateful to the U.S. Coast Guard?

7. Name one thing Steve's brother did while Steve was missing.

Part C FOLLOWING STRUCTURE. Answer the following questions on a separate piece of paper. You may look back at the story.

8. What is the full name of the "sailor" mentioned in line 13?

9. To what does "it" (line 26) refer?

10. What is the full name of the person referred to by "himself" (line 110)?

11. To whom does the "she" (line 144) refer?

Part D IDENTIFYING THE SEQUENCE OF EVENTS. Below are some events from the story. On a separate piece of paper, list the numbers. To the right of the number of the event that occurred first, write "A." To the right of the second one, write "B," etc. Try to answer without looking back at the story.

12. *Solo* sank in the Atlantic.

13. Local fishermen found Steve on the raft.

14. Steve caught a dolphin.

15. Steve built *Solo*.

16. Steve spent a day in the hospital.

Part E IDENTIFYING THE AUTHOR'S PURPOSE. Answer the following question on a separate piece of paper without referring to the story.

17. Which of the following best describes the author's main purpose?

   A. To expose Steve Callahan as being insane for sailing alone.
   B. To report a factual story from the point of view of the sailor's wife.
   C. To show that the Coast Guard sometimes uses poor judgment in cases such as this one.

Part F DISCUSSING YOUR REACTIONS AND INSIGHTS. Consider these questions for possible discussion in the classroom.

18. If you were related to Steve, what would you have done while he was missing at sea? Would your behavior be more like that of his wife, brother, or mother?

19. Do you think that Steve's experiences would make good material for a whole book? A full-length movie? Explain.

Prereading Activities
POSTAL SERVICE FOR CIVILIAN POW'S IN GERMANY

Part A MAKING PREDICTIONS.   You will be reading a true story that has the title given above. A "POW" is a prisoner-of-war. A "civilian" is someone who is not part of the military. Using your hunches, predict why thousands of British civilians were imprisoned on German soil during the war. Specifically, what were they doing in Germany during wartime?

Part B UNDERSTANDING NEW WORDS.   Below are scrambled definitions of words used in the story you are about to read. Unscramble the definitions by rearranging the phrases. Phrases are separated by double slashes (//). Then write a sentence using each word.

1. **retaliate** (verb) back // to pay // to being injured // in response

2. **intern** (verb) and confine // to detain // country // within // or definite area

3. **appalling** (adjective) horror, shock, // causing // or dismay

4. **alleviate** (verb) make // hard // to // less // to bear

5. **affix** (verb) or attach // fasten // to

6. **philatelist** (noun) studies // collects and // one who // stamped envelopes, etc. // postage stamps, postmarks,

7. **confiscate** (verb) to // private // seize // usually by a // property, // government or someone in power

Part C FOCUSING YOUR READING.   Now read the story. While you read, think about how you would have felt if you had been a civilian POW in Germany at the time that the events took place.

POSTAL SERVICE FOR CIVILIAN POW'S IN GERMANY

When England declared war on Germany in 1914, many people were caught by surprise, particularly the Germans who lived in or were visiting England and the British doing likewise in Germany.

The German government, upon hearing rumors of Germans being mistreated in England, warned the British to release these persons.

This warning was ignored, and the German government retaliated by interning the British in Germany.

A prisoner-of-war camp was set up outside Berlin. Prisoners were housed in the horse stalls, and the living conditions were appalling.

More than 4,000 prisoners were crammed into 11 barracks.

Later, an additional 12 barracks were built, but this did not do much to alleviate the problem.

In order to survive, the British prisoners had to find some way to overcome the wretched conditions. They began to organize the camp into a miniature England.

They formed societies, elected officials and even established an opera company. Shops were set up along a wall of the barracks, which became known as Bond Street.

In 1915, it was decided that the prisoner-of-war camp needed a postal service for internal mail, and a proposal was submitted to the German authorities.

This proposal was approved and Albert Kamps was appointed the "postmaster general." Kamps also was responsible for the external mail.

The postal service was started on July 18, 1915, and the post office sold stamps and postal stationery to prisoners.

At first, cards that required the affixing of adhesive stamps were issued. Soon the service was issuing postal cards, paid reply cards, letter cards and envelopes with imprinted stamps.

In his role as postmaster general, Kamps made a major mistake. He sent a letter to K. Hobrecker, a philatelist in Berlin, giving details of the postal service.

Hobrecker published this letter in a philatelic magazine in 1915.

This brought the postal service to the attention of the Berlin Philatelic Club, and members of the club issued a protest to the German government stating that the service was in violation of a law which prohibited local posts in Germany.

The prisoner-of-war postal service was forced to cease operations on April 3, 1916.

The remainders of postal stationery and stamps were confiscated and presumably destroyed.

Because of the small number of stationery items issued and used, these items are extremely rare.

The Higgins & Gage *World Postal Stationery Catalog* lists and illustrates the stationery of the prisoner-of-war camp but gives no values for these items.

Source: Donna O'Keefe, "POW Delivery Service was Short-Lived," *Linn's Stamp News,* Sidney, Ohio, 1983. Reprinted by permission of the publisher.

Postreading Activities
POSTAL SERVICE FOR CIVILIAN POW'S IN GERMANY

Part A *CHECKING YOUR PREDICTIONS.*   The answer to the question in Part A of the *Prereading Activities* is that the British civilians were caught by surprise in Germany when England declared war on Germany.

Was your prediction correct?

Part B *REMEMBERING FACTS.*   Answer the following questions by writing "T" for "true" or "F" for "false" on a separate piece of paper. Rewrite each false statement to make it a true statement. Try to answer without looking back at the story.

T   F   1.   About 40 prisoners were crammed into 11 barracks at first.

T   F   2.   The POW's established an opera company.

T   F   3.   The POW's established their own postal service.

T   F   4.   Members of the Berlin Philatelic Club wrote a letter to the POW's wishing them well with their postal service.

T   F   5.   The POW's postal service lasted for less than one year.

T   F   6.   Germany had a law that prohibited local posts.

Part C *IDENTIFYING THE SEQUENCE OF EVENTS.*   Below are some events from the story. On a separate piece of paper, list the numbers. To the right of the number of the event that occurred first, write "A." To the right of the second one, write "B," etc. Try to answer without looking back at the story.

7.   The German government heard rumors that Germans were being mistreated in England.

8.   England declared war on Germany.

9.   The German government warned the British to release the Germans who were in England.

10.   Unused POW postal stationery and stamps were confiscated.

11.   Albert Kamps was appointed the "postmaster general."

146

Prereading Activities
NEW YORK SUBWAYS

Part A MAKING PREDICTIONS. The true story you are about to read begins with these words: "ON A WINTER'S DAY IN THE NEW YORK CITY SUBWAY, 36 FELONIES WERE REPORTED TO...." Using your hunches, answer the following questions.

1. Which of the following types of felonies probably occurred most often?

    A. robbery   B. assault (attack on a person)   C. purse snatching

2. To whom were the felonies probably reported?

    A. the New York City newspapers
    B. the New York City Police Department
    C. the transportation system's own police force

Part B UNDERSTANDING NEW WORDS. Below are scrambled definitions of words used in the story you are about to read. Unscramble the definitions by rearranging the phrases. Phrases are separated by double slashes (//). Then write a sentence using each word.

3. **inebriate** (noun) person // a // drunken

4. **miscellaneous** (adjective) mixed kinds // various or // consisting of

5. **derelict** (noun) by society // a person // without a home // and rejected // or regular job

6. **labyrinth** (noun) arrangement of // a complicated // passages // winding

7. **dilapidated** (adjective) into disrepair // pieces or // falling to

8. **deranged** (adjective) or insane // mentally unstable // being

9. **intact** (adjective) with // or injured // missing // nothing

Part C FOCUSING YOUR READING. Now read the story. While reading, look for the one point in the story that would make you the most fearful if you were to ride the subway.

12. A philatelist published a letter from Kamps.

13. A protest was issued to the German government by a group in Berlin.

Part D DISCUSSING YOUR REACTIONS AND INSIGHTS. Consider these questions for possible discussion in the classroom.

14. How would you have felt if you had been a civilian POW in Germany at the time that the events took place? What one thing would have bothered you most?

15. Why do you think the POW's established a "miniature England"?

NEW YORK SUBWAYS

New York

On a winter's day in the New York City subway, 36 felonies were reported to the transit police: Eighteen people were robbed, six purses snatched, two people assaulted, two pockets picked, one wallet lifted, one sleeping inebriate rolled. Three felonies were listed as "miscellaneous." And there were three hat snatchings.

A female derelict was struck and killed by a train while walking on the tracks north of Times Square, tying up rush-hour traffic for two hours.

Rush-hour service in the labyrinth of lines serving lower Manhattan was snarled by a bomb scare. Two trains were halted when someone pulled an emergency cord and half a dozen others stacked up behind them. Vandals smashed windows on two dozen cars.

How much new graffiti was scrawled on subway cars went unreported.

On that same day, the New York City subway system carried 3.2 million passengers to and from their destinations safely and without incident. Those who defend the subways contend that's the bottom line.

New York subways—dirty, noisy, unsafe— are a Johnny Carson joke, a showpiece of urban America's decay. "Unsafe," grabs the headlines. Subway crime in January was up 60 percent over January of the previous year, and even Richard Ravitch, who heads the Metropolitan Transportation Authority, says he won't let his sons ride at night.

Cars, stations, maps and signs are buried under ribbons of spray-painted scrawls and curlicues. Stations are smelly and crumbling, signs and maps confusing, platforms dark and dangerous. Service is erratic—one of 10 cars is out of service at any given time. Passengers wait 20 minutes for a train, then two arrive within a minute. The subway scares and frustrates many New Yorkers and terrifies outsiders.

But that dilapidated, inefficient, scary subway also makes New York livable. One reason New Yorkers grumble about it so often is that they depend upon it so much.

New York is about the only place in the United States where owning a car is unnecessary. You can go almost anywhere on the subway. New York can skimp on school buses; students get free subway rides. Operating seven days a week, 24 hours a day, it carries a billion riders a year—more than any system in the world and more than the combined total of all other American subways except Chicago's have carried in their histories.

The subway system is a small kingdom. Its $1.5 billion operating budget is larger than those of 16 states. It employs 47,000 people, including a 3,300-member police force. It has 750 miles of track in total, 230 miles of passenger routes, 458 stations.

The system's 6,300 cars (more than the combined total of all other urban and commuter systems in the United States) transport bankers

and lawyers, clerks, machinists, housewives, 64
journalists. subway employees. It harbors the 65
impoverished, the deranged and the inebriated. 66
For some, a subway car is home. 67

About 250 people die on the tracks each 68
year, some accidentally. Most of them are 69
suicides who leap in front of trains. 70

Subway officials estimate that vandals smash 71
2,500 windows a month. Mischief-makers pull 72
emergency cords on trains or power switches 73
three times a day. Several million people a year 74
jump over or crawl under turnstiles, feed slugs 75
into them or simply walk through unattended 76
gates to beat the 75-cent fare. 77

More than 15,000 felonies were reported 78
last year and transit police issued 235,000 79
summonses for violations like smoking or radio 80
playing on trains. In January, the Transit Authority 81
cracked down on slug users: 10 of the first 32 82
people arrested were city employees. 83

As a mode of travel, the New York subway 84
is statistically safer than air or highway. 85

The last passenger fatality was in 1970, 86
when two people died in a train collision. They 87
were the first since 1928, when 16 were killed in 88
a derailment in Times Square. The worst disas- 89
ter was in 1918—97 people killed when a train 90
sped around a curve into a wall at Malbone 91
Street in Brooklyn. 92

Transit Authority executives contend the 93
subway is part of a larger problem. Subway 94
crime is about 2 to 3 percent of citywide crime, 95
meaning about one in 40 crimes is committed 96
underground. 97

Officials point out that crime figures are 98
often misleading. "Is our rate high or low? I don't 99
know," says John Simpson, president of the 100
Transit Authority. "The crime rate all over is 101
high, period," says James B. Meehan, chief of 102
the Transit Police. 103

Much of the problem is psychological. Eula 104
Mae Kelly, a cleaning woman who lives in 105
Brooklyn, has been mugged half a dozen times 106
in the past decade—always on the street. But 107
she always tries to take the bus rather than the 108
subway. 109

"I get scared down there," she says. "If I'm 110
on the street, I can yell or I can run. If I'm in one 111
of those cars, I feel like I'm trapped." 112

A man who works in Manhattan and lives in 113
Brooklyn Heights, the first stop in Brooklyn, 114
once fell asleep on his way home after midnight 115
and was carried on a nearly empty train to the 116
end of the line. The train was halfway back to 117
Manhattan when he awoke, at dawn, amazed to 118
find himself and his wallet still intact. 119

"It never occurred to me that under those 120
circumstances I could escape getting ripped 121
off," he says. 122

Meehan contends that New Yorkers fear 123
the subway because they more readily identify 124
with crime there. 125

"It's everybody's neighborhood. If you live 126
in Brooklyn and you read about some crime in 127
the Bronx, you dismiss it. If it occurs on the 128
subway and you ride the subway, you think 'this 129
could happen to me,' " he says. 130

"So you see some big guy get on the train, 131
looking threatening. He rides 10 stops and he 132
gets off and nothing happens. But that doesn't 133
change your perception." 134

For about a year, the Transit Authority has 135
been running an advertising campaign urging 136
passengers to take simple safety steps: don't 137
ride in empty cars; stand near token booths 138
while waiting; safeguard wallets and purses. 139
Some 400 new police have been hired. Prose- 140
cutors in Manhattan and Brooklyn are putting 141
special emphasis on subway crime. 142

None of that can guarantee safety. 143

Source: Dave Goldberg, "New York Subways," Associated Press, 1982. Reprinted by permission of the publisher.

Postreading Activities
NEW YORK SUBWAYS

Part A CHECKING YOUR PREDICTIONS. These are the answers to Part A of the *Prereading Activities:* 1. A, 2. C

Which ones did you get right?

Part B REMEMBERING FACTS. Answer the questions on a separate piece of paper. Try to answer without looking back at the story.

1. What was the female derelict doing just before she was killed?

2. Does the subway system carry thousands, millions, or billions of passengers on a given day?

3. Why are the maps and signs in the subway hard to read?

4. How many hours a day does the subway system operate?

5. What is the main reason why hundreds of people die on the tracks each year?

6. Is air, highway, or subway travel safest?

7. About what percent of all New York City crime occurs in the subways?

8. Name a safety step for passengers that the Transit Authority recommends.

Part C FOLLOWING STRUCTURE. Answer the following questions on a separate piece of paper. You may go back to the story.

9. To what does "it" (line 44) refer?

10. To what does "them" (line 76) refer?

11. What is the full name of the person speaking in lines 110 through 112?

12. What is the job of the man named in line 123?

13. To what does "it" (line 126) refer?

Part D IDENTIFYING MAIN IDEAS.   Answer each question by selecting the best choice. You may refer to the story.

14. Which of the following best expresses the main idea of the eleventh paragraph (line 61-67)?

    A. Some people live in the subway system.
    B. The system serves all kinds of people.
    C. The system has thousands of cars.

15. Which of the following best expresses the main idea of the next-to-last paragraph (lines 135-142)?

    A. Passengers need to take safety steps to avoid crime.
    B. Hundreds of new police will help reduce the crime rate.
    C. Officials are taking steps to deal with crime in the subways.

Part E DISCUSSING YOUR REACTIONS AND INSIGHTS.   Consider these questions for possible discussion in the classroom.

16. Tell what one thing would make you most fearful if you were in the subway. Explain why.

17. Speculate on some of the reasons why so many people ride the New York Subway System despite all its problems.

18. Suggest at least one method for reducing crime on the subway system other than the ones mentioned in the article.

Prereading Activities
THE VULTURES RETURN TO GETTYSBURG:
A LOCAL LEGEND AND A GRIM REMINDER

Part A MAKING PREDICTIONS.   You will be reading a true story that has the title given above. Gettysburg was the site of a huge, bloody battle during the Civil War. Using any hunches you may have, predict what the legend says.

Part B UNDERSTANDING NEW WORDS.   Below are scrambled definitions of words used in the story you are about to read. Unscramble the definitions by rearranging the phrases. Phrases are separated by double slashes (//). Then write a sentence using each word.

1. **watershed** (noun) that affects // a crucial turning point // opinion, etc. // action,

2. **awesome** (adjective) a mixed feeling of // inspiring // fear and wonder

3. **macabre** (adjective) and // both grim // horrible

4. **sentinel** (noun) or animal // a person // set to guard something // that is

5. **carrion** (noun) of a // dead body // the decaying flesh

6. **glacial** (adjective) a glacier // produced by // like or

7. **initiate** (verb) or use // into practice // to bring

8. **carcass** (noun) of an // the dead // animal // body

Part C FOCUSING YOUR READING.   Now read the story. While you read, think about whether you personally think that the legend might have some truth to it.

THE VULTURES RETURN TO GETTYSBURG:
A Local Legend and a Grim Reminder

Gettysburg, PA

Black vultures glide over the battlefield here. They circle high and swoop low over monuments and silent cannon, then move on to roost in tall trees overlooking the valley of a small stream called "Plum Run," where much of the bloodiest fighting of the Civil War took place.

Here was the watershed battle of that war—in only three days of fighting, 51,000 men from the North and South were killed, wounded, captured or missing.

Today more than a thousand stone and bronze monuments scattered throughout the battlefield tell their awesome stories, while overhead soar the macabre birds, grim sentinels of the past.

Hundreds of vultures winter here each year. Local legend has it that the large carrion-eating birds have been coming in great numbers for 120 years, ever since the three-day battle that began on July 1, 1863.

In January, researchers representing universities from the North and South began studying the black and turkey vultures to try to determine, among other things, whether the Civil War legend has basis in fact.

The vultures roost in a half-square-mile area in a mature forest set in the triangle formed by a steep rocky hillside known as "Little Round Top," a nearby forested higher rise called "Big Round Top" and a tangled maze of giant glacial boulders, the "Devil's Den."

Some of the heaviest fighting was here. Plum Run, which flows between "Devil's Den" and the Round Tops, became known as "Bloody Run."

One afternoon recently, a dozen vultures circled over "Devil's Den," where separate monuments note that Robertson's Brigade of Texas with the 3rd Arkansas Infantry captured the 4th New York artillery after three hours of hard fighting that ended at 5 p.m. on July 2, 1863.

The vultures circled the monuments for a few minutes, then returned to their nearby roost up amid wild grapevines that wind into the tops of ancient white pine, oak and ash trees. So many of the birds roost there that their droppings cover the ground like a heavy dusting of snow across the forest floor.

"It is kind of a romantic myth that these birds are part of the battle of Gettysburg," Harold J. Greenlee, natural resources specialist at Gettysburg National Military Park, said. "Scientifically, it is a speculating myth."

"They have wintered here for as long as anyone locally can remember," Greenlee said. "Part of what we are looking for in the study and why it was initiated is, 'Why Gettysburg? Why this battlefield area?' "

"We have one of the largest wintering populations of black vultures and turkey vultures in the eastern United States," Greenlee said. "The National Audubon Society's local chapter did a winter bird count last year and counted 870 birds here."

He became interested in the Gettysburg vultures through his work to restore the battlefield lands to what they were 120 years ago. With the help of John Karish, a national park service regional scientist, a study of the vultures was begun.

Others took interest, and now, aided by the U.S. Fish and Wildlife Service, the National Park Service and the Eastern National Park Monument Association, the two year study will include research by graduate students from Pennsylvania State University and Virginia Polytechnic Institute.

The Penn State study is being conducted by Dr. Richard H. Yahner, assistant professor of wildlife management with the university's School for Forest Resources, and Dr. Gerald L. Storm, assistant professor of wildlife management with the federal wildlife service.

"It's speculative," Yahner said, "but the interesting thing, and you almost have to say it tongue-in-cheek, is that some people say they are there as a consequence of the battle in 1863. We are trying to determine why they are using the park, what physical or vegetative features are attracting them to that area and not some other area."

Turkey vultures spend summers as far north as New England and Canada and in the winter go as far south as Florida. Black vultures exist from Pennsylvania south to the Falkland Islands off Argentina.

Since vultures live about 30 years, there would have been several generations of vultures since the battle.

Speculating on their connection with the battle, Yahner said, "Tradition may be something that is attracting them there. Everything depends on tradition. What is good for one generation is good for another. What was good in 1863 is good today."

In the three-day battle at Gettysburg, the Confederates lost 28,000 men of the 75,000 General Robert E. Lee had led north, while Union Army General George Gordon Meade lost 23,000 of his 88,000 soldiers.

There were also thousands of horses killed, as well as cattle of nearby farmers.

Soldiers of both sides buried their dead almost immediately after the fighting stopped. "They were even buried at night," John Heiser, Gettysburg National Park assistant research historian, said. "Soldiers from different regiments would go out and look for their own dead and wounded."

Vultures were likely attracted to the battlefield by the carcasses of 8,000 horses. "The army just left them," Heiser said. "It eventually wound up that the farmers in the area dragged them together in big piles and burned them, a few days to a few weeks after the battle."

Source: Joseph A. O'Brien, "The Vultures Return to Gettysburg," *The Hartford Courant,* 1983. Reprinted by permission of the publisher.

156

Postreading Activities
THE VULTURES RETURN TO GETTYSBURG:
A LOCAL LEGEND AND A GRIM REMINDER

Part A CHECKING YOUR PREDICTIONS. The answer to Part A of the *Prereading Activities* is that the legend says that the vultures have been coming to the battleground ever since the three-day battle that began on July 1, 1863.

Part B REMEMBERING FACTS. Answer the questions on a separate piece of paper. Try to answer without looking back at the story.

   1. In what state in the U.S. did the battle take place?

   2. What is the name of the war in which the battle occurred?

   3. To what does the term "Plum Run" refer?

   4. How far south do turkey vultures migrate?

   5. About how long does a vulture live?

   6. According to a research historian, vultures were probably attracted to the battlefield by the carcasses of what type of animal?

Part C FOLLOWING STRUCTURE. Answer the following questions on a separate piece of paper. You may go back to the story.

   7. To what does "they" (line 2) refer?

   8. To what does "there" (line 49) refer?

   9. To what does "it" (line 60) refer?

   10. To what does "it" (line 89) refer?

   11. To what does "them" (line 128) refer?

Part D IDENTIFYING MAIN IDEAS. Answer each question by selecting the best choice. You may go back to the story.

   12. Which of the following best expresses the main idea of the paragraph that begins on line 52?

      A. The birds are attracted to the Gettysburg National Military Park.

B. It's a speculating myth that the birds are part of the battle of Gettysburg.

C. Harold J. Greenlee is natural resources specialist at the park.

13. Which of the following best expresses the main idea of the paragraph that begins on line 62?

    A. The park has one of the largest wintering populations of black vultures and turkey vultures.

    B. Black vultures and turkey vultures are common in the eastern United States.

    C. A group did a winter bird count and counted 870 vultures in the park.

14. Which of the following best expresses the main idea of the paragraph that begins on line 74?

    A. The complete study of the vultures will take two years.

    B. Graduate students from two different universities will help with the study.

    C. Several agencies and institutions have joined in the study.

15. Which of the following best expresses the main idea of the paragraph that begins on line 123?

    A. The army left the dead horses behind.

    B. Farmers in the area put the dead horses in large piles and burned them.

    C. Vultures may have been attracted to the area by the large number of dead horses.

Part E DISCUSSING YOUR REACTIONS AND INSIGHTS. Consider these questions for possible discussion in the classroom.

16. Do you think it is likely that the legend has some truth to it? Why?

17. Speculate on why the author calls the birds "macabre."

18. Speculate on why some people are especially attracted to the study of birds. Are you? Why?

Prereading Activities
UNSUNG HERO KEEPS DANGEROUS FEDERAL HIGHWAY OPEN

Part A MAKING PREDICTIONS. You will be reading a true story that has the title given above. The story takes place in a small town located high in Colorado's mountains. Using this information, the information in the title, and any hunches you may have, answer each question in a sentence or two.

1. What probably makes the highway dangerous?

2. What has the person probably done to make himself a hero?

PART B UNDERSTANDING NEW WORDS. Below are words used in the story you are about to read. List them on a separate piece of paper. To the right of each, write its meaning, selecting from the scrambled list.

Word

3. disgorge
4. jurisdiction
5. gauge
6. fanfare
7. equate

Meaning (listed in scrambled order)

A. distance between the rails of a railway
B. territory or area of authority
C. to empty; to pour forth its contents
D. to think of as equal or closely related
E. noisy or showy display

Complete each of the following sentences by substituting one of the prereading words for the blank. The sentences are not part of the story but are given to help you understand the new words. (Do NOT write on this page. Rewrite the sentences on a separate piece of paper.)

8. There are few narrow _____ railways still in use in the United States.

9. It was difficult to _____ the hard look on his face with his kind words.

10. Because he was shy, he tried to avoid the _____ they were making over his accomplishment.

11. Her _____ included all the countries in the southern part of the state.

12. If you tip the beehive, it will _____ all the bees.

Part C FOCUSING YOUR READING. Now read the story. While you read, think about whether you would like to have the hero's job. Why?

UNSUNG HERO KEEPS DANGEROUS FEDERAL HIGHWAY OPEN

Silverton, CO

Every time Lynn Watson goes to work, he 1
puts his life on the line for $13 an hour and 2
calls himself a happy man. 3

He is paid by people he doesn't know, to 4
perform a service they take for granted, in a 5
place where, by the laws of nature, they 6
shouldn't be. 7

He is a highway man who measures his 8
years in winters and his months in blizzards. 9
His job is to live 9,300 feet above sea level in 10
southwestern Colorado and to keep a 17- 11
mile stretch of U.S. Highway 550 open for the 12
driving public. 13

Watson's territory is one of the most 14
dangerous sections of paved federal road in 15
the United States. There are 18 major ava- 16
lanche areas between the 11,018-foot summit 17
of Red Mountain Pass on the west and the 18
10,901-foot summit of Molas Pass on the east- 19
ern boundary of Watson's jurisdiction. Hair- 20
pin turns and thousand-foot dropoffs are 21
commonplace. Midway through this winter, 22
there was enough snow to bury a two-story 23
building. 24

But Connie Watson claims, "I'm one of 25
the few women in the world who can hon- 26
estly say my husband loves his job." 27

For the past nine years, she and Lynn 28
have raised their three sons in a government- 29
issue house in this old Colorado mining town 30
of 800 people. 31

Silverton is a nest of rainbow Victorian 32
houses dwarfed by mile-high towers of ice 33
and rock. At first glance, it looks like the town 34
clock should have stopped in 1905. But sur- 35
rounding mines and the famous narrow gauge 36

Durango to Silverton railroad, which disgorges 37
thousands of tourists in the summer, have 38
kept Silverton on the map. 39

During seven solid months of winter, the 40
mailman frequently brings in the milk and 41
bread, too. Locals joke about the town's zero 42
population growth, because there is no doc- 43
tor in Silverton and the nearest hospitals are 44
in Montrose, 61 miles to the north, or 45
Durango, 50 miles to the south; both are 46
reached via U.S. 550. 47

There are no school buses, so children 48
take their sleds to class and then slide home 49
for lunch. Some winters get so fierce resi- 50
dents give up trying to plow out their front 51
doors. Instead, they just step out of their 52
second-story windows onto the hard-packed 53
snowdrifts. 54

"Frankly, I wouldn't care if I never saw 55
another snowflake again," says Mrs. Watson, 56
a cheerful 39-year-old teller at the local bank. 57
"But Silverton is a wonderful place to live 58
because of the people. And although Lynn's 59
is the only name on the paycheck, we all feel 60
that we're a part of what he does." 61

She says the Watson boys each grew up 62
learning how to work the ever-present com- 63
munications radio in the kitchen, "and 64
watching the weather, waiting for Dad to 65
come in from the storm. The weather con- 66
trols Lynn's job, and his job controls our 67
lives." 68

Yet, Watson considers himself an ordi- 69
nary person performing a job he was trained 70
to do without much fanfare. He doesn't 71
equate his work with courage or sacrifice as 72

he and his machines and men disappear in a 73
blizzard at midnight when the thermometer 74
registers 20-below. 75

Born 41 years ago in the tiny southwest- 76
ern Colorado village of Rico, Watson has 77
spent all his life living above 8,000 feet. He 78
started working in the mines while still a teen- 79
ager, and nearly 20 years ago he hired on as a 80
part-time highway man in nearby Quray to 81
supplement his winter income. 82

In 1967 he became a certified Colorado 83
civil servant and went full time with the State 84
Highway Department. He was appointed senior 85
man in Silverton in 1973 and now oversees a 86
crew of two in summer and four in winter. 87

The keys to Watson's business are steel- 88
nerved men and finely honed machines. The 89
tools are mammoth—snow-plowers, snow 90
throwers, bulldozers, graders and trucks. The 91
snow throwers chew tons of white stuff at a 92
gulp and spit the stream 150 feet out of the 93
roadway. Bulldozers open slide areas too 94
bulky for lesser machines. 95

"Everybody has to know how to run 96
everything," says Watson. "I enjoy working 97
on the equipment, keeping it tip-top, but I 98
like being on the road a lot better. 99

"I'd be lying if I said I'd never been afraid 100
in a snowstorm, but mostly I just don't think 101
about it, I'm so intent on getting the job 102

done. I think that more than being afraid of 103
the weather, we all respect it. 104

"But the worst times are at night, when 105
you can't see what's above you and you're 106
clearing a slide area. You wonder if it's all 107
going to come in on top of you." 108

Occasionally, when avalanches or white- 109
outs threaten death, Watson advises his bosses 110
to close the only link between Silverton and 111
the rest of the world. But in emergencies, he 112
braves the arctic conditions himself. Three 113
times, he's led an ambulance over the moun- 114
tains to reach help for an injured miner, a 115
heart attack victim and a patient in insulin 116
shock. 117

And it was on just such a night that he 118
clomped his snow-caked boots through the 119
back door, swept his waiting dinner off a 120
plate and onto a piece of tin foil, then 121
disappeared without a word. 122

"I was mad and I was worried, all at the 123
same time," says Mrs. Watson. 124

"Our youngest son, Mark, put his arm 125
around me and said, 'Don't worry, Mom, you 126
know Dad always comes home.' And he 127
always does, even if it's 24 hours later." 128

Watson adds with a grin: "I've never 129
fallen off the mountains, but I've had a wheel 130
or two hanging off the edge." 131

Source: Tad Bartimus, "Unsung Hero Keeps Dangerous Federal Highway Open," Associated Press, 1982. Reprinted by permission of the publisher.

Postreading Activities
UNSUNG HERO KEEPS DANGEROUS FEDERAL HIGHWAY OPEN

Part A CHECKING YOUR PREDICTIONS. These are the answers to Part A of the *Prereading Activities:* 1. The snow and ice on the twisting highway make it dangerous. 2. During bad winter weather, he's kept the highway open most of the time and has helped people with medical emergencies get through to help.

Which of your predictions were on the right track?

Part B REMEMBERING FACTS. Answer the following questions by selecting the best choice for each. Try to answer without looking back at the story.

1. The hero is responsible for a stretch of federal highway that is about how many miles long?

   A. 17   B. 57   C. 550

2. Does the hero like his job?

   A. yes   B. no   C. The author give no hint.

3. The name of the town in which the hero lives is

   A. Durango   B. Silverton   C. Montrose

4. During the winter months, the mail carrier helps by

   A. running snow plowing equipment on the highway

   B. bringing information he heard on his communications radio

   C. bringing bread and milk to the town

5. In addition to using snow removal equipment on the road, what else does the hero do as part of his job?

   A. He runs the local radio station from his house.

   B. He removes snow from the driveways of the old Victorian houses.

   C. He works on the equipment to keep it in good condition.

6. What is the hero's main feeling when he thinks about the weather?

   A. fear   B. respect   C. dislike

Part C FOLLOWING STRUCTURE. Answer the following questions on a separate piece of paper. You may go back to the story.

7. What is the first name of the "husband" (line 27)?

8. Who is the "we" referred to in line 60?

9. To what does "it" (line 102) refer?

Part D IDENTIFYING MAIN IDEAS. Answer the following questions on a separate piece of paper. You may go back to the story.

10. In the fourth paragraph (lines 14-24), which sentence (1st, 2nd, 3rd, or 4th) best expresses the main idea of the paragraph?

11. In the eleventh paragraph (lines 62-68), which sentence (1st or 2nd) best expresses the main idea of the paragraph?

Part E DISCUSSING YOUR REACTIONS AND INSIGHTS.   Consider these questions for possible discussion in the classroom.

12. Would you like to have Lynn Watson's job? Why?

13. What image of the town is brought to your mind by the author's use of the phrase "nest of rainbow Victorian houses" in line 32?

14. Name at least two specific dangers Lynn faces on the job, and tell how you personally would feel about facing each one.

15. Speculate on what inspires a person to do life-threatening work.

Prereading Activities
SO YOU WANT TO BE A SANTA CLAUS

Part A *MAKING PREDICTIONS.*   You will be reading a true story that has the title given above. It's about a school that teaches applicants how to act as Santas when employed by stores. The following questions are answered in the story. Using your own experiences and any hunches you may have, answer each question. After you've read the story, check your answers.

1. Is Santa allowed to say "Ho, ho, ho"?

2. Must a Santa wear gloves?

3. What should Santa say if a child wants Santa to "bring Mommy and Daddy back together" after their divorce?

Part B *UNDERSTANDING NEW WORDS.*   Find the following words in the story on the lines listed below. Do not read the whole story yet, just the paragraph in which each word appears. Try to determine the meanings of the words from context. List the words on a separate piece of paper and define each.

4. dilemmas (line 15)
5. girth (line 22)
6. amenity (line 22)
7. anteroom (line 31)

8. appraising (line 33)
9. belligerent (line 93)
10. discharge (line 94)

Part C *FOCUSING YOUR READING.*   Now read the entire story. While you read, think about whether you would personally like to work as a Santa in a department store. Why?

SO YOU WANT TO BE A SANTA CLAUS

San Francisco

It's a West Point for Santas, and with Christmas 1
all but upon us, it's time for a little brushup of the 2
white chemical beard and a quick quiz: 3

You're a Santa Claus, and the little kid on your 4
lap says there's only one thing she wants for Christ- 5
mas: She'd love mommy and daddy to get back 6
together. What do you say? 7

Or how about: The kid doesn't say anything, 8
and merely, as they put it at Santa West Point, "has 9
an accident." 10

For which of the following offenses can a Santa 11
Claus be fired: shoplifting, being drunk on the job, 12
saying "Ho, ho, ho"? 13

The answers to these and other recurring yule- 14
tide dilemmas are provided at Western Temporary 15
Services, Inc., a national organization that says it has 16
provided more Santas to private employers than 17
anyone in the world. 18

The free school is located at 572 Market Street. 19
When you walk in, you find a glass-and-fern- 20
decorated lobby with a quick elevator to the second 21
floor. For Santas—given their girth—the amenity is 22
appreciated. 23

Upstairs wait half a dozen aspiring Saint Nicks, 24
all looking for a job. The pay is $4 an hour, $4.25 if 25
you complete the job. One Santa leafs through an 26
electronics catalog; another glances at a few pages in 27
Esquire. Then a young woman comes in and says the 28
first class is about to begin. 29

Forget Donner and Blitzen. The Claus cadets 30
have to hoof it on their own to a small anteroom, 31
while the service's other employees look on with, let's 32
say, appraising smiles. 33

To start fast, the young woman in charge says, 34
"We don't say 'ho, ho, ho.' We've found that 'ho, ho, 35
ho' frightens children." 36

In a few moments, you'll learn the right thing to 37
say instead, see a training film, do role plays and learn 38
how to become wonderful Santas. 39

From now on, she says, you won't be addressed 40
by your name. You'll be called "Santa." Then she 41
introduces Jenny Zink, from the national organization. 42

Zink is thin, chic, businesslike—a worthy repre- 43
sentative of Western Temporary Services, Inc., for 44
whom she is western coordinator of the Santa 45
division. 46

First, she says, we'll have a training film. 47

The film is—and with Christmas coming on, 48
who could lie?—outstanding. A woman who looks 49
like the heroine of a 1950s private-eye movie gives 50
the word on how to handle the tough ones, the kid 51
who kicks you in the shins or pulls your beard. (That 52
answer is classified.) 53

Dependability and punctuality are primary 54
because so many people are counting on you, the film 55
says. 56

If a child asks you for a little brother or sister or 57
to bring parents back together, tell the child that you 58
only bring toys. 59

Don't recommend brand-name toys, but do 60
recommend brushing teeth, eating vegetables and 61
drinking milk. Parents appreciate that. 62

Memorize the names of Santa's reindeer. Some 63
kids will ask you as a test. 64

If a child throws up or has an accident in your 65
lap, try to handle the incident diplomatically. Quietly 66
return the child as quickly as possible (Western owns 67
the Santa Claus suits) and take a brief break. Some 68
Santas wear plastic shields, the film notes. 69

Both the film and Jenny Zink remind the Santa 70
cadets to remember during their breaks to stay out of 71
sight of the children "if you remove your beard or 72
costume." 73

The plastic beard is flammable, the students are 74
warned, so don't smoke. 75

"And remember Santa is married, so no flirting." 76

Students are reminded not to discuss politics, 77
religion or social issues and to remember that 78
personal hygiene is important. 79

"We like to think Santa bathes daily and uses 80
cologne or aftershave as well as deodorant," the pri- 81
vate eye's pal says. Mouthwash helps too. 82

At the end of the film, there's time for questions. 83
The would-be Kris Kringles seem to be a bright lot; 84
they've followed the film with interest, and all seem 85
ready to fill those plum jobs at the Emporium, Macy's 86
and Pier 39. 87

They've learned the "Santa lift" that helps bring 88
kids to your lap without courting back trouble, heard 89
that state law requires wearing thick white gloves at 90
all times while handling children (Western provides 91
three pairs that are to be washed daily) and learned 92
that shoplifting, drinking, being mean or belligerent 93

or just being indifferent are all grounds for discharge. 94

Two of the Claus cadets are brothers, Willie and 95
Ronnie Banks, husky Florida emigres who have 96
played clown in front of their father's furniture store 97
back home. They've been working in a candle factory 98
and figure the change of pace will be great. 99

When Zink asks for volunteers, Ronnie offers 100
Willie and within minutes a perfectly normal-looking 101
San Francisco resident turns into a candy-ad Santa 102
Claus. The plastic beard, the suit that fits anyone from 103
a size 36 to 54 thanks to a drawstring and pillow, the 104
plastic white wig, a cap that is to be worn at a rakish 105
angle—all work their magic. Willie will make a 106
superb Santa Claus. 107

That means that he and his brother will get one 108
of the best Christmas presents available—a job—and 109
bring a lot of joy to San Francisco Bay Area kids who 110
come to see them. They also probably will have a lot 111
of fun and some great stories to tell. 112
Merry Christmas. 113

Source: Jim Wood, "So You Want to Be Santa Claus," *The San Francisco Examiner,* 1979. Reprinted by permission of the publisher.

Postreading Activities
SO YOU WANT TO BE A SANTA CLAUS

Part A CHECKING YOUR PREDICTIONS.   These are the answers to Part A of the *Prereading Activity:* 1. No, Santas are not supposed to say "Ho, ho, ho." 2. Yes, by state law a Santa must wear gloves while handling children. 3. The Santa should say that he only brings toys.

Which of your predictions were correct?

Part B REMEMBERING FACTS.   Answer the following questions by writing "T" for "true" or "F" for "false" on a separate piece of paper. Rewrite each false statement to make it a true statement. Try to answer without looking back at the story.

T   F   1.   Compared with other temporary services that provide Santas, the one described in this story is the largest.

T F 2. The pay for being a Santa is $4.25 an hour if the Santa completes the job.

T F 3. According to the author, the training film is a little silly.

T F 4. The plastic beard is flammable.

T F 5. The temporary service provides five pairs of gloves.

T F 6. The suit provided by the temporary service fits a wide range of sizes.

T F 7. The author ends the story with the sentence, "Consider being a Santa next Christmas."

Part C DRAWING INFERENCES.   Use everyday reasoning skills to answer the following questions with either a "yes" or "no." Be prepared to explain the reasoning you used to reach each answer.

8. Are Santas probably told they will receive more money per hour if they complete the job in order to discourage them from quitting?

9. Is the waiting Santa who leafs through an electronics catalog while waiting for training probably trying to learn more about electronic toys so he can discuss them with children?

10. Are there probably "back-up" Santas at each store in case one doesn't show up or is late?

11. Is the statement "We like to think Santa bathes daily ..." (line 80) probably a gentle hint to the Santas in training?

12. Is it probably easier to prove that a Santa has been drinking on the job than it is to prove that the Santa has been "mean"?

13. Do very young children probably notice that Santa's beard is made out of plastic?

14. Does the author believe that the cadets will find the job to be fascinating?

Part D IDENTIFYING MAIN IDEAS.   Answer each question by selecting the best choice. You may go back to the story.

15. Which of the following best expresses the main idea of the paragraph that begins on line 48?

A. People avoid telling lies at Christmas.

B. The woman looks as if she's from the 1950's.

C. The film is quite good.

16. Which of the following best expresses the main idea of the paragraph that begins on line 83?

A. The would-be Santas are bright and interested in the job.

B. Most of the would-be Santas want to work at either the Emporium, Macy's or Pier 39.

C. Would-be Santas are allowed to ask questions during training.

Part E DISCUSSING YOUR REACTIONS AND INSIGHTS.   Consider these questions for possible discussion in the classroom.

17. Would you personally like to work as a Santa in a department store? Why?

18. What are some probable reasons why some department stores hire Santas through an employment agency rather than directly hiring and training the Santas themselves?

19. Speculate on the reasons why the answer to handle the tough ones (such as those children who kick you) is classified.

Answers

Snake Attempts to Eat Master

PREREADING ACTIVITIES

PART A See Part A of Postreading Activities in your book.

PART B 4. very large, nonpoisonous snakes that crush their prey to death

       5. having ugly or mean tendencies

       6. a person in charge of a museum, library, etc.

       7. the branch of zoology having to do with the study of reptiles and amphibians

POSTREADING ACTIVITIES

PART A Note: This part refers to Part A of the Prereading Activities.

PART B 1. 14 feet

       2. live rabbits

       3. snake teeth

       4. four

       5. Jacksonville Zoo

       6. ax and knife

PART C 7. Boggess

       8. pythons or snakes

       9. J. Bennett Boggess

PART D   10.   B

PART E   Answers will vary.

Explorer's Lifetime Goals List: It's 108 Down, Only 19 to Go

PREREADING ACTIVITIES

PART A   See Part A of Postreading Activities in your book.

PART B	1.	B		9.	whimsy
	2.	C		10.	cremation
	3.	H		11.	elite
	4.	D		12.	precocious
	5.	F		13.	circumnavigate
	6.	A		14.	anthropologist
	7.	G		15.	inept
	8.	E		16.	suffice

POSTREADING ACTIVITIES

PART A   Note: This part refers to Part A of the Prereading Activities.

PART B	1.	A		6.	C
	2.	B		7.	B
	3.	B		8.	C
	4.	B		9.	B
	5.	B			

PART C	10.	line 26
	11.	line 53
	12.	line 71
	13.	line 75
	14.	line 91

PART D	15.	B
	16.	A
	17.	C
	18.	D

PART E   Answers will vary.

How Celebrities Recall Their First Dates

PREREADING ACTIVITIES

PART A   See Part A of Postreading Activities in your book.

PART B   1.   a person who specializes in the study of mental and emotional processes and their effects on behavior

2.   belief in one's own abilities

3.   a man's tailless jacket for evening wear

4.   the story of one's own life written by oneself

POSTREADING ACTIVITIES

PART A   Note: This part refers to Part A of the Prereading Activities.

PART B   1.   Johnny Carson

2.   Joyce Brothers

3.   read library books

4.   went to his house to sing

5.   continued to the dance; his jacket hid the split

6.   brown

7.   He put his arm around her.

8.   Magic Johnson

9.   Lucille Ball

PART C   Exact wording and answers may vary.

10.   probably friendly because he was willing to mention the letter to a reporter

11.   at least 39, since she met him when he was 14 and she hasn't seen him in more than 25 years (14 + 25 = 39)

12.   Phyllis Diller, because she says she had "a pimple the size of Australia" on her nose

13.   Liberace, because he named the piano teacher he had when he was four years old

PART D   Answers will vary.

A Book to Swat Roaches With:
They May Be Brainless, But They're Not Stupid

PREREADING ACTIVITIES

PART A   See Part A of Postreading Activities in your book.

PART B   2.   an indefinitely long period of time

3.   a remnant or trace of an organism that lived in a past age such as a skeleton or a footprint in the earth's crust

4.   any chemical that is used to kill insects and rodents

5.   a small piece or bite of food

6.   at the very beginning

7.   implied or understood although not directly expressed

POSTREADING ACTIVITIES

PART A   Note: This part refers to Part A of the Prereading Activities.

PART B   Note: Exact wording may vary.

1.   cockroaches

2.   no

3.   three weeks

4.   Africa

5.   head for high ground

6.   increase their activity

7.   toenails or paper or soap or toothpaste

PART C   8.   line 1

9.   line 18

10.   line 35

11.   line 46

12.   line 51

PART D   Note: Answers and wording may vary.

13.   because they may contain cockroaches, which you may bring into your home

175

14. because poisonous spray may get on things, and thus you might get poisoned

15. getting rid of cockroaches entirely from the earth

PART E   Answers will vary.

A Former Beauty Queen: 'There's Life After Size 10'

PREREADING ACTIVITIES

PART A   See Part A of Postreading Activities in your book.

PART B   Allow for variations in wording of meanings.

3. public presentation, often showy and colorful

4. starting

5. a group that travels and works together, often entertainers

6. tryout for a position or job

7. a business that represents workers, finds them work, etc.

8. without name; not recognized or known

POSTREADING ACTIVITIES

PART A   Note: This part refers to Part A of the Prereading Activities.

PART B   1. Texas

2. 34

3. "Just make sure it's really large."

4. worked out twice a day

5. Joan Crawford

6. Bob Hope

7. just to accompany a friend

8. She's a former Miss Texas.

9. Butler (Note: Her name became Blaylock after she got married, which was after becoming Miss Texas.)

10. T-shirt

11. Joan Crawford

12. her extra weight

13. Kim Dawson

PART D 14. B   17. C

         15. A   18. D

         16. E

PART E   Answers will vary.

Finding Those Fascinating Facts

PREREADING ACTIVITIES

PART A   See Part A of Postreading Activities in your book.

PART B   1. A   4. B

         2. C   5. A

         3. A   6. C

POSTREADING ACTIVITIES

PART A   Note: This part refers to Part A of the Prereading activities.

PART B   1. F   (Ancient Greek and Roman vessels did not have a "fore" or "aft"; they were sharp at both ends.)

         2. F   (Living human brains are lavender or pink.)

         3. T

         4. F   (The term "saint" originally applied in the New Testament to all believers.)

         5. F   (The fastest-growing racial group in the U.S. is Asian.)

         6. T

         7. T

         8. F   ("Walla, walla" is an Indian term meaning "many waters.")

         9. T

PART C   Note that there may be variations in wording.

10. Probably not, because he says that he learned the fascinating facts "en route to looking up other things."

11. Probably not, because that continent has half the world's refugees although it only has 10 percent of the world's population.

12. Probably yes, because of the term "gray matter."

13. Probably not, since Isaac Newton is famous in history, and it is reasonable to infer that he is no longer living.

14. Probably yes, because Belgians have the largest and most spacious homes in the world—much larger than Russian homes.

PART D   Answers will vary.

Surprise Chess Contender: A 15-Year-Old Girl

PREREADING ACTIVITIES

PART A   See Part A of Postreading Activities in your book.

PART B   Allow for variations in wording of meanings.

1. one with much experience

2. a contest with a number of contestants and a series of games

3. aware of

4. too much (overbearing) pride

5. to gather (together)

6. a regular course that goes from place to place

7. long lasting

POSTREADING ACTIVITIES

PART A   Note: This part refers to Part A of the Prereading Activities.

PART B   1. Washington, D.C.

2. Alaska

3. her father

4. the 12 top-rated players in the country

5. because she is a young girl

6. pushed the pieces off the board

7. while playing chess

8. $250 to $300

9. foreign languages

PART C 10. D 13. C

11. B 14. E

12. A

PART D 15. B 17. C

16. A 18. B

PART E Answers will vary.

The Little Cat That Could

PREREADING ACTIVITIES

PART A See Part A of Postreading Activities in your book.

PART B Allow for variations in wording of meanings.

1. a member of the cat family

2. one who brings up another's child

3. to renew; to train to overcome a handicap

4. difficult situation

5. help out

6. to make up for

7. damages

8. short accounts, usually of true events

POSTREADING ACTIVITIES

PART A Note: This part refers to Part A of the Prereading Activities.

PART B 1. eight weeks

2. San Francisco

3. to give refuge, rehabilitation and placement to homeless animals

4. They were moving to a house where pets were not allowed.

5. onions and potatoes

6. no

7. Helen Keller and "The Kitten"

PART C 8. line 9
9. line 9
10. line 40
11. line 80
12. line 99

PART D Since these questions require inferences, allow for some differences of opinion.

13. yes

14. yes

15. no

PART E Answers will vary.

The Sweet Art of Jellybean Mosaics

PREREADING ACTIVITIES

PART A See Part A of Postreading Activities in your book.

PART B
1. A
2. B
3. A
4. B
5. C
6. A
7. C
8. C
9. C

POSTREADING ACTIVITIES

PART A Note: This part refers to Part A of the Prereading Activities.

PART B
1. F (Peter Rocha lives in San Francisco.)
2. T
3. F (The media has given Rocha's art a lot of attention, including coverage on TV, in newspapers, and in magazines.)
4. T

5. T

6. F (Rocha is a native of San Antonio, Texas.)

7. F (To survive financially, Rocha must continue his graphic arts and illustration business.)

8. F (Each mosaic takes about a week to finish.)

PART C Note that wording may vary.

9. The media is interested in and excited about Rocha's jellybean art.

10. Rocha has to supplement his income from jellybean art with income from his business.

11. Rocha is interested in continuing his work, but doesn't know where it will lead.

PART D Note that wording may vary.

12. They are very attracted to it.

13. The interest in his work was beyond reasonable proportions.

14. All the attention and publicity happened so fast that it's hard to keep track of.

15. finish

16. someone who isn't exactly like everyone else

PART E Answers will vary.

Echo: A Victim of Animal Abuse

PREREADING ACTIVITIES

PART A See Part A of Postreading Activities in your book.

PART B Allow for variations in wording of meanings.

1. cared for and helped

2. springing back; resistant to being held down

3. jailed

4. the condition of being kept or guarded

5. receiver of benefits

6. dog (member of the family of dogs)

7. a place for the care of the sick

8. famous, celebrated

POSTREADING ACTIVITIES

PART A   Note: This part refers to Part A of the Prereading Activities.

PART B   1. San Francisco

2. because her owner was arrested

3. man

4. Someone called because Echo had been left tied to a parking meter for a long time.

5. Cinderella Fund

6. a job as a Hearing Dog

PART C   7. animals (who are victims of animal abuse)

8. animals (who are rescued in time from animal abuse)

9. Echo

10. Echo's owner

11. Echo's owner

12. Echo

13. Echo's foster parent

14. Demonstration Hearing Dogs

15. Echo

PART D 16. good

17. bad

18. good

19. good

20. good

PART E   Answers will vary.

Gains and Losses for American Women

PREREADING ACTIVITIES

PART A   See Part A of Postreading Activities in your book.

PART B	1. G	10. remobilize
	2. B	11. spearhead
	3. H	12. deputy
	4. A	13. equity
	5. E	14. correspondent
	6. F	15. flex
	7. I	16. ratification
	8. D	17. aeronautics
	9. C	18. tactic

POSTREADING ACTIVITIES

PART A   Note: This part refers to Part A of the Prereading Activities.

PART B   1. 35

2. 1972

3. to turn anti-ERA politicians out of office and to elect more women in seats in the state legislatures

4. National Organization for Women

5. installed the first woman as president of the National Press Club

6. Columbia College

7. humorous material

8. union

9. elect the first woman to be president of the club

10. line 7
11. line 29
12. line 38
13. line 58
14. line 66
15. line 79

PART D   Because inferences are required, allow for differences of opinion.

16. no

17. no

18. no

19. no

20. no

PART E   Answers will vary.

The Care and Feeding of Superstitions

PART A   See Part A of Postreading Activities in your book.

PART B   Allow for variations in wording of meanings.

1. not well known
2. to relate to
3. supporters
4. to grow or increase in size
5. to shrink or decrease in size
6. put into (water or liquid)

POSTREADING ACTIVITIES

PART A   Note: This part refers to Part A of the Prereading Activities.

PART B   1. T

2. F (Some of the superstitions are obscure.)

3. F (You must eat duck on Easter Sunday or you will be unable to pay debts.)

4. T

5. F (When you find two kernels, you're supposed to eat one and throw the other over your head and make a wish.)

6. F (Norse gods retained their strength and youth by eating apples.)

PART C   7. superstitions

8. eggs

9. second piece of mince pie

10. fruit that is out of season

11. the other kernel in a nut

12. the apple

PART D   Answers will vary.

Collecting Garbage for Fun and Fame

PREREADING ACTIVITIES

PART A   See Part A of Postreading Activities in your book.

PART B   Allow for variations in wording of meanings.

1. given up
2. gone wild
3. rubbish
4. bent
5. take air in
6. happening over a long period of time
7. something that transports such as a truck, car, etc.

POSTREADING ACTIVITIES

PART A   Note: This part refers to Part A of the Prereading Activities.

PART B
1. Berkeley
2. garbagemen (line 47)
3. self-respect
4. summer
5. They don't eat well or much.
6. jog
7. nicer people live there
8. give it to the dogs

PART C
9. the rest of the crew
10. Luis Rodriquez
11. Wild Bill, Super Chicken, Billy Polk, and Louis Blane
12. Fred Neal
13. the job garbagemen do
14. Mashin' Mike Ayers
15. the can's owners
16. the garbageman
17. the sanitation company

18. his work as a garbageman

19. people who live in the flats

20. neighborhood dogs

21. people in this country

PART D Allow for variations in wording.

22. No, but he has to push himself.

23. reputation

24. probably to lead a good life, have pride in their work, provide for their families, and be happy

25. probably contain used cans and bottles of alcoholic beverages and little else; probably little garbage from food

26. probably high quality

27. stick it out

PART E Answers will vary.

Abie Nathan's War on War Toys

PREREADING ACTIVITIES

PART A Note: See Part A of Postreading Activities in your book.

PART B 4. C   8. profit
5. B   9. ceremony
6. D   10. incredulous
7. A   11. aggressive

POSTREADING ACTIVITIES

PART A Note: This part refers to Part A of the Prereading Activities.

PART B 1. toy tanks OR toy pistols OR toy guns

2. Minister of Education

3. none

4. $1 million

5. He bought them from shops.

6. one

PART C 7. a child's (a Jewish child's)

           8. Israel

           9. toy stores

         10. toy stores other than Sifri

PART D Answers will vary.

Getting It Stuck to You—and Loving It

PART A See Part A of Postreading Activities in your book.

PART B 1. E   7. calisthenics

           2. D   8. skeptical

           3. B   9. deteriorate

           4. F   10. chemotherapy

           5. C   11. excruciating

           6. A   12. herniated

POSTREADING ACTIVITIES

PART A Note: This part refers to Part A of the Prereading Activities.

PART B 1. the Beatles

           2. Los Angeles, California

           3. William Holden OR James Coburn, OR James Garner, OR William Shatner, OR Merv Griffin, OR Jane Fonda, OR Natalie Wood, OR Peggy Lee

           4. stimulates energy flow through them

           5. no

           6. every two weeks

           7. a few minutes

           8. removed her drug side-effects

PART C 9. acupuncture

         10. George Harrison

         11. Zion Yu

         12. acupuncture

         13. Larry Sears

14. Maurice Zolotow
15. Thelma Walker

PART D   16. line 25
17. line 39
18. line 68
19. line 96
20. line 108

PART E   Answers will vary.

Dick Gregory Starves to Aid Hunger Fight

PREREADING ACTIVITIES

PART A   See Part A of Postreading Activities in your book.

PART B   1. to check systematically in order to collect certain types of information
2. the ability to recover from illness, change, etc.
3. fine food prepared by highly skilled chefs
4. to break down food so it can be used
5. a physician who studies and treats nonsurgical internal diseases

POSTREADING ACTIVITIES

PART A   Note: This part refers to Part A of the Prereading Activities.

PART B   1. New Orleans
2. Dick Gregory
3. political reasons
4. taking salt pills
5. pictures of hamburgers, haute cuisine, and nature scenes
6. body fat
7. every morning
8. walk to Baton Rouge

PART C   9. Dick Gregory
10. Dick Gregory

11. hunger strike

12. Dick Gregory's metabolism

13. Irish

14. Dr. Len Simon

PART D 15. C

16. A

17. A

18. A

PART E   Answers will vary.

A Food Sampler of Strange Things to Eat

PREREADING ACTIVITIES

PART A   See Part A of Postreading Activities in your book.

PART B   1. an abundance of food often displayed in a goat's horn

2. relating to a kitchen or to cookery

3. having the charm of the unfamiliar

4. a statement that is often long and repetitive

5. not impaired or cut up in any way

6. tasting or smelling strong and sharp

7. the sense of taste

POSTREADING ACTIVITIES

PART A   Note: This part refers to Part A of the Prereading Activities.

PART B   1. C   8. B

2. B   9. B

3. B   10. hostess

4. A   11. writer

5. A   12. ducks' tongues (as food)

6. B   13. snake soup

7. C   14. the chile pepper

PART D 15. first

16. first

17. second

PART E Answers will vary.

A Noah's Ark Survival Plan for Imperiled Species

PREREADING ACTIVITIES

PART A See Part A of Postreading Activities in your book.

PART B
1. C
2. G
3. A
4. H
5. B
6. D
7. E
8. F

9. obstacle
10. habitat
11. innovative
12. curator
13. inbred
14. propagate
15. collaboration
16. criteria

POSTREADING ACTIVITIES

PART A Note: This part refers to Part A of the Prereading Activities.

PART B
1. two
2. because some cannot reproduce in captivity
3. 30
4. 250
5. $4,000
6. having a rancher maintain a breeding herd of Grevy's zebra and black rhino for participating zoos
7. inbreeding, which led animals to lose their genetic characteristics

PART C
8. zoos
9. Elvie Turner, Jr.
10. William Conway
11. female antelopes
12. Elvie Turner, Jr.

PART D 13. line 30
        14. line 44
        15. line 63
        16. line 79

PART E Answers will vary.

Charlie Parkhurst: The Stagecoach Driver with a Secret

PREREADING ACTIVITIES

PART A See Part A of Postreading Activities in your book.

PART B 2. B   11. veer
        3. D   12. comply
        4. A   13. fledgling
        5. E   14. dub
        6. F   15. taciturn
        7. H   16. ironic
        8. G   17. wiry
        9. C   18. insulate
        10. I   19. bane

POSTREADING ACTIVITIES

PART A Note: This part refers to Part A of the Prereading Activities.

PART B 1. T
        2. F (He grudgingly gave in to the highwayman the first time.)
        3. T
        4. F (He was five feet, seven inches tall.)
        5. F (Charlie was taciturn.)
        6. F (The "Concord" was a type of stagecoach.)
        7. F (He would drink some after a run but never before or during one.)
        8. T
        9. F (He retired because he lost the sight of one eye.)
        10. F (Charlie died in 1879.)

PART C 11. "Throw down the box."

  12. the highwaymen on their horses

  13. Charles D. Parkhurst

  14. Tuolumne River Bank

  15. Charlie Parkhurst

  16. stagecoach wheels

  17. Charlie's friends

POSTREADING ACTIVITIES

PART D 18. B

  19. A

PART E Answers will vary.

Not Pretty at Any Speed: Being an Inspector at a Chicken Cutting Plant

PREREADING ACTIVITIES

PART A See Part A of Postreading Activities in your book.

PART B	1.	B		9.	entrails
	2.	A		10.	decibel
	3.	C		11.	tedious
	4.	F		12.	peruse
	5.	D		13.	postmortem
	6.	E		14.	shackles
	7.	G		15.	carcass
	8.	H		16.	contamination

POSTREADING ACTIVITIES

PART A Note: This part refers to Part A of the Prereading Activities.

PART B	1.	B		5.	A
	2.	A		6.	C
	3.	B		7.	A
	4.	C			

192

PART C   8.   line 16

           9.   line 43

       10.   line 80

       11.   line 99

       12.   line 134

PART D   Exact wording and answers may vary for some questions.

13. United States Department of Agriculture

14. probably because it takes less time since the chicken does not have to be turned around

15. probably because it takes less time and because they work so closely together over time, the gestures are readily understood

16. probably a scandal when people start getting bad chickens (and perhaps getting ill) because the chicken-inspecting process is becoming too quick to be perfectly accurate

17. because packers want the inspections done quickly and may want inspectors to overlook "bad" chickens

PART E   Answers will vary.

20   Andrew Hallidie—The Canny Cable Car Inventor

PREREADING ACTIVITIES

PART A   See Part A of Postreading Activities in your book.

PART B   Allow for variations in wording of meanings.

3. someone who is new to a country

4. causing horror or shock

5. something that carries objects and/or people

6. not discouraged

7. persistent, not giving up

8. government permit

9. luxurious and expensive

10. cannot be imitated or copied

POSTREADING ACTIVITIES

PART A   Note: This part refers to Part A of the Prereading Activities.

PART B   1.   T
         2.   T
         3.   T
         4.   F (He got assistance from investors.)
         5.   F (On the first run, it ran at 8 miles per hour.)
         6.   F (The cable car quickly became a financial success.)
         7.   T

PART C   8.   San Francisco
         9.   investors
        10.   a new part or apparatus that was needed
        11.   problems (in building the cable car)
        12.   cable car routes
        13.   the cable car

PART D 14.   A
        15.   C
        16.   B
        17.   D
        18.   E

PART E   Answers will vary.

21 Julia Morgan: The Architect Behind the Castle

PREREADING ACTIVITIES

PART A   See Part A of Postreading Activities in your book.

PART B   1.   E   10.   H
         2.   A   11.   I
         3.   F   12.   unobtrusive
         4.   D   13.   relegated
         5.   K   14.   credo
         6.   G   15.   rustic
         7.   B   16.   exhilarating
         8.   C   17.   grandiose
         9.   J   18.   instill

19.	shun	21.	patron
20.	incredulity	22.	anomaly

POSTREADING ACTIVITIES

PART A　Note: This part refers to Part A of the Prereading Activities.

PART B	1.	1920s and 1930s	5.	burned down
	2.	14	6.	no
	3.	Paris	7.	California
	4.	Mills College	8.	the castle

PART C	9.	C	14.	A
	10.	A	15.	B
	11.	E	16.	B
	12.	B	17.	C
	13.	D		

PART E　Answers will vary.

22　The Giants Are Going Home

PREREADING ACTIVITIES

PART A　See Part A of Postreading Activities in your book.

PART B　Allow for variations in wording or meanings.

1. hard to find or see
2. large sea animals
3. known to few
4. things needed
5. trying to gain the love or affection of another
6. compete
7. those who break rules or laws
8. exploring journeys
9. bound to happen
10. high-spiritedness; great joy

POSTREADING ACTIVITIES

PART A Note: This part refers to Part A of the Prereading Activities.

PART B 1. California Gray Whale
2. their oil
3. 17,000
4. late December
5. They are pregnant females.
6. $20
7. bobbing
8. flip their tails
9. It's fun to spend the day on the boat or beach.

PART C 10. the migration
11. an art
12. the migration
13. the whales

PART D Allow for some differences of opinion.

14. good
15. good
16. bad
17. good
18. good

PART E Answers will vary.

23 Idiot Savant: The Extraordinary Sculpture of a Retarded Artist

PREREADING ACTIVITIES

PART A See Part A of Postreading Activities in your book.

PART B Allow for variations in wording or meanings.

3. suitable
4. a good example; a model of its kind.

5. to handle with skill

6. strange or causing wonder

7. strong and healthy

8. to care for

9. to take unfair advantage of

24 POSTREADING ACTIVITIES

PART A   Note: This part refers to Part A of the Prereading Activities.

PART B   1. F (He had the social skills of a six-year-old.)

2. F (He only attends two or three shows a year.)

3. T

4. T

5. T

6. T

7. T

8. F (He is a part-time artist and a full-time stableboy.)

PART C   9. Alonzo Clemens

10. Alonzo's

11. Jim Graves

12. his work

PART D 13. A

14. B

PART E   Answers will vary.

25 New Delhi is Talking About Child Marriage

PREREADING ACTIVITIES

PART A   See Part A of Postreading Activities in your book.

PART B   3. needing careful handling, tact, etc.

4. prohibited by custom or law

5. support or encouragement given by a person or group

6. suggestive of future success or luck

7. unaware or forgetful of something

8. having limited knowledge, experience, or culture

9. seeming probable or very likely

POSTREADING ACTIVITIES

PART A   Note: This part refers to Part A of the Prereading Activities.

PART B 1. B   4. A

         2. B   5. A

         3. B

PART C 6. line 6   8. line 37

         7. line 28   9. line 55

PART D Answers will vary.

26 Making Paper for Making Money

PREREADING ACTIVITIES

PART A   See Part A of Postreading Activities in your book.

PART B 1. C   4. C

         2. A   5. A

         3. C   6. C

POSTREADING ACTIVITIES

PART A   Note: This part refers to Part A of the Prereading Activities.

PART B 1. Massachusetts

         2. 180 years

         3. cotton

         4. It's a solidifying agent.

         5. no

         6. no

         7. throwaway paper collars

PART C 8. line 7   11. line 77

         9. line 23 12. line 83

       10. line 60

PART D 13. probably to prevent robberies

14. probably because some people in those countries don't like the United States and would be unhappy if they learned that the paper for their money was made in the U.S.

15. probably since they are the only contractor for U.S. money, and they have other contracts and goods being sold.

PART E Answers will vary.

27 Man Returns After 76 Days on Raft

PREREADING ACTIVITIES

PART A See Part A of Postreading Activities in your book.

PART B 3. behaving calmly under suffering, bad fortune, etc.

4. gentle and good-natured

5. evidence that points to the probability of something

6. any difficult, painful, or trying experience

7. any wandering or extended journey

8. water-dwelling mammals with numerous teeth and often beaklike snouts

POSTREADING ACTIVITIES

PART A Note: This part refers to Part A of the Prereading Activities.

PART B 1. Maine

2. *Napoleon Solo*

3. 2,000

4. one day

5. being hit by a whale or another boat

6. no

7. contacted all shipping lines that had vessels traveling where Steve could be found OR alerted ports and planes OR called radio stations OR maintained communications between himself and his parents and Frisha

PART C 8. Frisha Callahan

9. something in the sea (the rubber life raft)

10. Edd Callahan
11. Frisha

PART D 12. B   15. A
          13. D   16. E
          14. C

PART E 17. B

PART F Answers will vary.

28 Postal Service for Civilian POW's in Germany

PREREADING ACTIVITIES

PART A See Part A of Postreading Activities in your book.

PART B 1. to pay back in response to being injured
          2. to detain and confine within a country or definite area
          3. causing horror, shock, or dismay
          4. to make less hard to bear
          5. to fasten or attach
          6. one who collects and studies postage stamps, postmarks, stamped envelopes, etc.
          7. to seize private property, usually by a government or someone in power

POSTREADING ACTIVITIES

PART A Note: This part refers to Part A of the Prereading Activities.

PART B (Note: Exact wording may vary.)

          1. F (About 4,000 prisoners were crammed into 11 barracks at first.)
          2. T
          3. T
          4. F (Members of the Club issued a protest against the postal service.)
          5. T
          6. T

PART C	7.	B	11.	D
	8.	A	12.	E
	9.	C	13.	F
	10.	G		

PART D Answers will vary.

New York Subways

PREREADING ACTIVITIES

PART A See Part A of Postreading Activities in your book.

PART B 3. a drunken person

4. consisting of various or mixed kinds

5. a person without a home or regular job and rejected by society

6. a complicated arrangement of winding passages

7. falling to pieces or into disrepair

8. being mentally unstable or insane

9. with nothing missing or injured

POSTREADING ACTIVITIES

PART A Note: This part refers to Part A of the Prereading Activities.

PART B (Note that exact wording may vary.)

1. walking on tracks

2. millions

3. hidden by spray paint

4. 24

5. suicides

6. subway

7. 2 to 3

8. don't ride in empty cars OR stand near token booths while waiting OR safeguard wallets and purses

PART C 9. subway

10. turnstiles

11. Eula Mae Kelly
12. Chief of Transit Police
13. subway

PART D 14. B
15. C

PART E Answers will vary.

The Vultures Return to Gettysburg:
A Local Legend and a Grim Reminder

PREREADING ACTIVITIES

PART A See Part A of Postreading Activities in your book.

PART B 1. a crucial turning point that affects action, opinion, etc.
2. inspiring a mixed feeling of fear and wonder
3. both grim and horrible
4. a person or animal that is set to guard something
5. the decaying flesh of a dead body
6. like or produced by a glacier
7. to bring into practice or use
8. the dead body of an animal

POSTREADING ACTIVITIES

PART A Note: This part refers to Part A of the Prereading Activities.

PART B 1. Pennsylvania
2. Civil War
3. a small stream
4. Argentina
5. 30 years
6. dead horses

PART C 7. black vultures
8. tops of the trees
9. the study
10. the legend
11. dead horses

PART D 12. B   14. C

13. A   15. C

PART E   Answers will vary.

Unsung Hero Keeps Dangerous Federal Highway Open

PREREADING ACTIVITIES

PART A   See Part A of Postreading Activities in your book.

PART B 3. C   8. gauge

4. B   9. equate

5. A   10. fanfare

6. E   11. jurisdiction

7. D   12. disgorge

POSTREADING ACTIVITIES

PART A   Note: This part refers to Part A of the Prereading Activities.

PART B 1. A   4. C

2. A   5. C

3. B   6. B

PART C 7. Lynn

8. the family

9. fear of the situation

PART D 10. 1st

11. 2nd

PART E   Answers will vary.

So You Want to Be a Santa Claus

PREREADING ACTIVITIES

PART A   See Part A of Postreading Activities in your book.

PART B   Allow for variations in wording or meanings.

4. difficult choices to be made

5. distance around something

6. something that increases one's physical comfort

7. waiting room

8. judging the value of something

9. warlike

10. release from service

POSTREADING ACTIVITIES

PART A   Note: This part refers to Part A of the Prereading Activities.

PART B   1. T

2. T

3. F (According to the author, the film is outstanding.)

4. T

5. F (The service provides three pairs of gloves.)

6. T

7. F (He ends it with "Merry Christmas.")

PART C   Since these require inferences, allow for some differences of opinion.

8.	yes	12.	yes
9.	no	13.	no
10.	no	14.	yes
11.	yes		

PART D   15. C

16. A

PART E   Answers will vary.